DON QUIXOTE: HERO OR FOOL?

Part II

by John J. Allen

A University of Florida Book

UNIVERSITY PRESSES OF FLORIDA
FAMU / FAU / FIU / FSU / UCF / UF / UNF / USF / UWF

Gainesville 1979

Library of Congress Cataloging in Publication Data   (Revised)

Allen, John Jay, 1932–
   Don Quixote, hero or fool.

   (University of Florida monographs. Humanities, no. 29, 46)
   Vol. 2 "A University of Florida book."
   Vol. 2 has imprint University Presses of Florida.
   Bibliographical footnotes.
   1. Cervantes Saavedra, Miguel de, 1547–1616. Don Quixote. I. Title. II. Series:
Florida. University, Gainesville. University of Florida monographs.
Humanities, no. 29 etc.
PQ6353.A4   863'.3   71–625420
ISBN 0–8130–0630–9 (v. 2)

University Presses of Florida is the central agency for scholarly publishing of the
State of Florida's university system. Its offices are located at 15 NW 15th Street,
Gainesville, FL 32603. Works published by University Presses of Florida are
evaluated and selected for publication by a faculty editorial committee of any one
of Florida's nine public universities: Florida A&M University (Tallahassee),
Florida Atlantic University (Boca Raton), Florida International University
(Miami), Florida State University (Tallahassee), University of Central Florida
(Orlando), University of Florida (Gainesville), University of North Florida
(Jacksonville), University of South Florida (Tampa), University of West Florida
(Pensacola).

PREFACE

This volume embodies the results of rereading and rethinking *Don Quixote* in the years since the writing of *Don Quixote: Hero or Fool?* (Gainesville: University of Florida Press, 1969). Many of the reviews were helpful to me, and this second part is due in large measure to E. C. Riley's comment that my monograph was "not half long enough" (*Hispanic Review* 39 [1971]: 453). Ruth El Saffar's review article ("Apropos of *Don Quixote: Hero or Fool?*," *MLN* 85 [1970]: 269–73) helped me to see that in my exposition of the reader's movement toward Don Quixote I had neglected the inversely corresponding movement away from the narrator, treated here in chapter 1. I do not, of course, mean to imply that these two *cervantistas* are in any way responsible for the contents of this volume. On the contrary, I must apologize to them for not having taken up other provocative challenges in their respective reviews.

I am also grateful to Juan Bautista Avalle-Arce and the fellows of the Southeastern Institute of Medieval and Renaissance Studies at Duke University for their inspiration and support during the summer of 1974, when I wrote chapter 1. I want to thank Robert A. Bryan, vice-president for academic affairs at the University of Florida, for making it possible for me to accept the fellowship at Duke. Final thanks go to the Graduate School of the University of Florida for making possible the publication of this monograph.

My primary concern here, as in my earlier study, is to clarify the reader's evolving relationship with the protagonist. Chapter 1 focuses upon the relationship between the reader and the narrator, chapter 2 upon the significance of the structural parallel between Don Quixote and Sancho for the reader-protagonist relationship, and chapter 3 upon the strategies of irony which relate all of the major characters to the novel's system of values. All three chapters complement and corroborate my earlier findings concerning the contextual and stylistic devices that disclose the proper ethical perspective on Don Quixote. Chapter 1, however, involves a radical reconsideration of the question of Cid Hamete's reliability. The three were planned from the outset as a coherent series, and only the length of time necessary for each investigation and the relative autonomy of each essay prompted me to publish the first two separately.

———•———

Chapter 1 is reprinted, with changes, from *Modern Language Notes* 91 (1976):201–12, by permission of the publisher. Copyright 1976 by the Johns Hopkins University Press. Chapter 2 is reprinted, with changes, from *Revista Hispánica Moderna* 38 (1974–75):141–52, by permission of the publisher. Copyright 1977 by the Hispanic Institute, Columbia University.

CONTENTS

For Luly and Tisha

1. THE NARRATORS, THE READER, AND DON QUIXOTE

From the Moors you could never hope for any word of truth, seeing that they are all of them cheats, forgers, and schemers.

Part II, Chapter III

The relationships established at the outset of *Don Quixote* between the narrator, the reader, and the protagonist are not difficult to characterize. The narrator's humility, openness, and lack of pretensions seem genuine. The ingratiating and flattering invitation to shared irony is very attractive to the reader, and the relationship quickly becomes quite close ("dearest reader," "gentle reader").[1] We easily and naturally adopt the attitude of ironic detachment held by Don Quixote's "stepfather"—a term which suggests just the right mixture of distance and control. But these relationships change significantly in the course of Don Quixote's adventures, and this change profoundly affects the way we interpret the novel.

In *Don Quixote: Hero or Fool?* (Part I), I attempted to show how Cervantes shifts the reader's attitude toward Don Quixote from one of derision to one of sympathy, respect, and admiration. The shift derives in part from such changes as Don Quixote's increasing cognizance of reality, his loss of control over events, the increase in deception practiced upon him, the element of self-doubt, the change in the ethical status of his antagonists, and the shift from emphasis upon physical prowess to emphasis upon strength of spirit.[2] Cervantes guides the process throughout—not simply the changes in Don Quixote and his circumstances, but also the reader's judgment of these changes: we implicitly accept the existence of a Moorish enchanter in the

1. *The Ingenious Gentleman Don Quixote de la Mancha*, trans. Samuel Putnam, pp. 11, 16. Subsequent references are to this translation. Italics within quotations from *Don Quixote* are mine throughout, and departures from the Putnam translation, at times for accuracy, at other times for precision, are also mine, and are in brackets and identified by an asterisk preceding the page reference, e.g., (*665).
2. *Don Quixote: Hero or Fool?* (Part I), p. 83.

3

world of the novel in Part II, Chapter II; chivalric archaism (a device used for the comic deflation of Don Quixote's rhetoric) disappears from his speech after Part II Chapter XXXII; the comic expectation of—and desire for—Don Quixote's defeat is consistently lacking after Part II, Chapter XLVIII.

Now, if the narrator and the reader begin the novel in close rapport, and both view the protagonist from a critical and ironic distance, and if in the course of the novel factors are introduced, as outlined above, which draw the reader nearer to the protagonist, one of two corollaries must follow: either the narrator accompanies the reader in the move toward the protagonist, or he does not, and the distance between narrator and reader correspondingly increases. Since in a coherent work of art the author and the reader must be assumed to share a common ethical perspective on the protagonist, this second alternative would seem to necessitate the introduction of a surrogate narrator. At least the alternative only becomes available when a surrogate narrator is introduced, or through some other process of authorial distancing.[3]

Ruth El Saffar has seen the character-author facet of this complex relationship most clearly: "Cervantes' tone in Chapter I is one of great irony implying an easy assurance of the profound gulf separating him, the storyteller, from Don Quijote, his clearly insane character. But as the outlines of this character begin to take on substance, Don Quijote begins to emerge as a threat to his author's integrity and distance. As Don Quijote becomes more sympathetic, Cervantes is threatened by assimilation with his character. The need to reassert control and distance is perhaps symbolized by the unexpected interposing of a fictitious historian."[4] Without wishing to diminish the importance of her remarks, I must take exception to some of the implications of Professor El Saffar's analysis. First, the idea that it is Don Quixote who moves Cervantes, rather than the other way

3. "The literary work of art is a communication and . . . the communicant is thereby guided and controlled, though not coerced, by its totality": Lowry Nelson, Jr., "The Fictive Reader and Literary Self-Reflexiveness," in *The Disciplines of Criticism*, ed. Peter Demetz et al., pp. 189–90.

4. "The Function of the Fictional Narrator in *Don Quijote*," p. 176.

around, threatens to revive, at a higher level of sophistication, the "lay genius" issue—the idea that Cervantes did not really understand what he had accomplished. And in any event, Cid Hamete is introduced long before I, at least, can detect any authorial activity in behalf of the shift in sympathies. Secondly, it seems to me that Cervantes need not have left behind a representative of the originally established distance as he and the reader begin to draw nearer to Don Quixote. That he did so is part of the uniqueness of the work compared to other novels of anagnorisis that involve a revised perspective on characters and events, such as those René Girard treats in *Mensonge romantique et vérité romanesque.*

As Don Quixote "becomes more sympathetic," Cervantes *and* the reader of course move toward him, but Cid Hamete does not. Cid Hamete *is* an unreliable narrator, as it is indicated early in the novel that he may be, but not because he does not keep his facts straight. His essential reliability in that respect is definitively established in Part II.[5] It is his perspective on Don Quixote that is unreliable, because it does not change as the character changes, and so Cervantes contrives to alienate the reader from him to counterbalance the movement toward Don Quixote. As Cervantes says: "Whenever he might and should deploy the resources of his pen in praise of so worthy a knight, the author appears to take pains to pass over the matter in silence" (73). An essential feature of the perspectivism of *Don Quixote* is the number of remarks that must be taken *both* ironically *and* literally, from different perspectives. This remark is quite properly taken ironically when it appears, but it acquires literal significance by the end of the novel.

Although Cid Hamete is Cervantes' predecessor in the fictional scheme of things, he is his successor in the actual narration, and he thus inherits the ironic perspective that is already clearly and solidly established by the time he first appears in Chapter IX. Cid Hamete's manuscript views Don Quixote from the same ironic

5. "No serious discrepancies emerge between [Don Quijote's and Sancho's] literary reputations [Part I] and their current selves in Part II": Edward C. Riley, "Who's Who in *Don Quijote*? Or an Approach to the Problem of Identity," p. 128.

perspective, although Cervantes is careful to dissociate himself from his successor by casting doubt upon his reliability.

Just as Cervantes speaks in the early chapters of "all the foolish things that Don Quixote said" (48), the Golden Age speech in Chapter XI is characterized by Cid Hamete as a "futile harangue" (82), and reference is made in the episode of Mambrino's helmet to his "mad, ill-errant thoughts of chivalry" (158). Since Cid Hamete's perspective on Don Quixote does coincide so exactly with that established by the implied Cervantes of Chapters I through VIII, and since there is usually no clear attribution to Cid Hamete or to Cervantes of the infrequent commentary after the introduction of the Moor, it might be supposed that it is Cervantes who comments throughout on Cid Hamete's text, but it is clear that a remark such as "Who would not have laughed at hearing the nonsense the two of them talked, master and man?" does indeed reflect the attitude of Cid Hamete, who calls Sancho and Don Quixote "[two fools]" (*964). The last characterization of Don Quixote directly attributable to Cervantes is made as Sancho sets out to take possession of Barataria, during the sojourn with the duke and duchess that marks the turning point in his career:[6]

> And now, gentle reader, let the worthy Sancho go in peace and good luck go with him. You may expect two bushels of laughter when you hear how he deported himself in office. Meanwhile, listen to what happened to his master that same night, and if it does not make you laugh, it will at least cause you to part your lips in an apelike grin; for Don Quixote's adventures are to be greeted either with astonishment [admiración] or with mirth. (790–91)

This commentary maintains the original perspective which Cid Hamete has been shown to share, yet there is just enough ambiguity in the word admiración to allow for a shift in Cervantes' perspective paralleling the reader's change in orientation. The chapters that follow this passage are, in fact, among the most decisive in the shift in sympathies.

6. See chap. 2, below, pp. 25–26.

Assuming for the moment, then, that Cervantes and his character Cid Hamete do not share the same perspective on the protagonist throughout the novel, let us examine some of the characteristics of the narration which can be seen as contributing to the alienation of the reader from the narrator.

The order of exposition in the novel is clearly attributable to Cid Hamete, as can be seen in such remarks as: "Here we shall leave them for the present, seeing that Cid Hamete would have it so" (913), and: "At this point Cid Hamete leaves him and goes back to Don Quixote" (869). One of the most striking differences in this respect between Parts I and II of the novel lies in the way in which information about characters and events is delivered to the reader.

Typical of the exposition in Part I is the presentation of the episode of Mambrino's helmet. The narrator explains Don Quixote's self-deception before the encounter takes place: "The truth concerning that helmet and the horse and horseman that Don Quixote had sighted was this: . . . [a] barber, . . . a brass basin, . . . an ass" (158). This is the pattern of all the adventures in Part I. There is no deception of the reader and very little mystery. In two episodes, the adventure of the fulling mills and the adventure of the corpse, the circumstances are not immediately clear, but things never seem to be other than what they are. In the whole involved introduction of Cardenio, Dorotea, Fernando, and Lucinda and the incremental advance of their relationships there is of course a great deal of mystery, but insofar as they participate in the deception of Don Quixote, the reader is always informed of the truth in advance.

In Part II, however, there are a number of exceptions to the pattern. The withholding of information begins very early: "Carrasco went to hunt up the curate and make certain arrangements with him which will be duly narrated when the time comes" (550). The reader is given no advance indication of the reality behind the abrupt appearance of the actors of *The Parliament of Death*:

> Don Quixote was about to make a reply but was interrupted by the sight of a cart crossing the highway, filled

with the most varied and weird assortment of persons and
figures that could be imagined. He who drove the mules and
served as carter was an ugly demon.... The first figure that
Don Quixote beheld was that of Death himself, with a
human countenance. (575)

The most significant examples of subsequent, as opposed to
prior, revelation are the two encounters with Sansón Carrasco,
as the Knight of the Mirrors (II, XII) and as the Knight of the
White Moon (II, LXVI), and the episode of Maese Pedro (II,
XXIV). There should be no question that this kind of limitation
on the reader's knowledge brings him closer to Don Quixote, for
do we not condescend to and stand aloof from him precisely to the
extent that we know, or think we know, more about reality than
he does? At the same time, we begin to move away from the
narrator, who knows in advance how each episode turns out, is
aware all along of the reality which these deceptions hide, and
chooses to exclude us from what was formerly our privileged
position beside him by means of "a 'presentación ilusionista,'
through which the reader replicates the experiences of the
character and, like him, is fooled or confused. . . . "[7]
It is more difficult to assess the effect of the two cases of
misinformation in Part II. (I am aware of none in Part I.) On the
one hand, we know that Cid Hamete is introduced with doubts
about his reliability, doubts that are echoed in Don Quixote's
reaction to the news of the appearance in print of Part I:

He was a bit put out at the thought that the author was a
Moor, if the appellation "Cid" was to be taken as an indication, and from the Moors you could never hope for any word
of truth, seeing that they are all of them cheats, forgers, and
schemers. (526)

On the other hand, we have the confirmation of the reliability of
Part I in Part II, the contrast drawn between Cid Hamete's
"true" Don Quixote and Avellaneda's false character, and Cer-

7. Francisco Rico, *La novela picaresca y el punto de vista*, p. 43. The translations from this and other cited critical works in Spanish are my own. "*Presentación
ilusionista*," as Rico notes, is Maria Rosa Lida de Malkiel's term. Cf. Edward C.
Riley, "*Don Quijote*," in *Suma cervantina*, pp. 65–71.

vantes' repeated insistence on the completeness and accuracy of the Moor's account:

> Cid Hamete Benengeli was a historian who was at great pains to ascertain the truth and very accurate in everything. (117)
>
> Really and truly, all those who enjoy such histories as this one ought to be grateful to Cid Hamete, its original author, for the pains he has taken in setting forth every detail of it, leaving out nothing, however slight, but making everything very clear and plain. He describes thoughts, reveals fancies, answers unasked questions, clears up doubts, and settles arguments. In short, he satisfies on every minutest point the curiosity of the most curious. (764)

Yet we discover two instances of deception in Part II. First, Cid Hamete tells the reader, of Countess Trifaldi, "that the lady's right name was the Countess Lobuna and that she was so called on account of the many wolves in her country" (756), though she is, of course, as he himself later reveals, a majordomo of the duke's. The second deception occurs during the governorship of Sancho, when a farmer, who is presented to us with the comment that "it could be seen from a thousand leagues away that he was a worthy man and a good soul" (813), later turns out to be a "rogue [who] knew how to play his part very well" (815).

It is true that both cases involve the introduction of minor characters and that the thrust of the first example probably goes outside the book, as a reference to the Osunas, but the second example certainly involves the same kind of withholding of information of which I have just spoken, compounded by deliberate deception.

Another contribution to the alienation of the reader from the narrator is made by the instances of "authorial" insensitivity which have led some readers to feel that Cervantes "hardens his pen" against his hero. Judgments here become more subjective, but an early example which seems to bother many readers comes near the end of Part I when Don Quixote is felled by one of the penitents and "Sancho . . . [flings] himself across his master's body ... weeping and wailing in the most lugubrious and, at the same time, the most *laughable* fashion that [can] be imagined" (456). I have myself suggested before that the reader rebels against Cid Hamete's comment at the close of the episode of the enchanted boat: "Don Quixote and Sancho then returned to their beasts and to [being] beasts" (*703).[8]

Is there not also perhaps a note of this insensitivity in the gratuitous clarification at the very end of the novel: "Don Quixote,... amid the tears and lamentations of those present... gave up the ghost; *that is to say, he died*" (987)?

Finally, allied to this insensitivity, there are authorial judgments—all in Part II—with which it seems to me the reader simply cannot agree. In the episode of the lions, for example, the encounter is introduced by Cid Hamete with fulsome praise for Don Quixote:

> O great-souled Don Quixote de la Mancha, thou whose courage is beyond all praise, mirror wherein all the valiant of the world may behold themselves, a new and second Don Manuel de León, once the glory and the honor of Spanish knighthood! With what words shall I relate thy terrifying exploit, how render it credible to the ages that are to come? What eulogies do not belong to thee of right, even though they consist of hyperbole piled upon hyperbole? (615)

But all this must be seen as ironic in the light of his later characterization of the encounter as a demonstration of "the extent of his unheard-of madness," and of Don Quixote's challenge to the lion as "childish bravado" (616). I do not believe that the reader accepts this characterization of Don Quixote's challenge. And he must also take exception to a remark in Chapter LXXI: "Dismounting at a hostelry, the knight recognized it for what it was and did not take it to be a castle ... ; *for ever since he had been overcome in combat he had talked more rationally* on all subjects. . ." (972). Don Quixote has not taken an inn for a castle in all of Part II, and Cid Hamete himself notes the change twice: "His master took it for a real inn this time and not for a castle

8. *Don Quixote: Hero or Fool?* (Part I), p. 45.

10

as was his wont" (671), and : "I say inn, for the reason that this was what Don Quixote called it, contrary to his usual custom of calling all inns castles" (893).

Perhaps the most striking example of reader disagreement with an authorial judgment involves the crucial episode of the Cave of Montesinos. Don Quixote had been hauled out of the cave,

> and when they had him all the way up they saw that his eyes were closed and that, to all appearances, he was sound asleep. They laid him on the ground and untied him, but even this did not wake him. It was not until they had turned him over first on one side and then on the other and had given him a thorough shaking and mauling that, after a considerable length of time, he at last regained consciousness, stretching himself as if he had been roused from a profound slumber and gazing about him with a bewildered look. (655)

After recounting the adventure, Cid Hamete makes the following comment in the margin of the text, explicitly addressed to the reader:

> I cannot bring myself to believe that everything set down in the preceding chapter actually happened to the valiant Don Quixote. . . . And so, without asserting that it is either false or true, I write it down. You, wise reader, may decide for yourself; for I cannot, nor am I obliged, to do any more. It is definitely reported, however, that at the time of his death [they say] he retracted what he had said, confessing that he had invented the incident because it seemed to him to fit in well with those adventures that he had read of in his storybooks. (*665–66)

The choice which Cid Hamete offers us, then, is to take the events of the cave either as actual fact or as a conscious lie on the part of Don Quixote. But the reader knows that it was neither. It was a dream. The terms of the novel as a whole preclude, of course, the possibility that the event was "real," and the lie option is definitively ruled out by the references during the rest of Part II to

Don Quixote's being "unable to make up his mind as to whether what had happened to him in the Cave of Montesinos was real or not" (739). The best commentary on Cid Hamete's lack of perception and sensitivity, and the judgment of the knight and his squire which ought most to offend the reader, is his characterization of the Don Quixote and Sancho of Chapter LXX of the Second Part as "[two fools]" (*964).

Cid Hamete, then, has kept the reader in the dark about a number of things, excluding him from the intimacy which Cervantes had established in the early chapters. He has occasionally misinformed him concerning the facts. He reveals an insensitivity to the changes in Don Quixote which have deepened the reader's attachment to the knight, and he makes judgments and conjectures about him which conflict with the facts of the account or with the reader's clear sense of what is appropriate.

Are we justified in insisting upon this distinction between Cervantes and Cid Hamete? Cervantes has told us not to trust Cid Hamete. E. C. Riley says that "the reader who seeks to pursue the intricacies of Cervantes' game with fact and fiction must try to keep a cool head—and on no account confuse Cid Hamete's story with the novel *Don Quixote* by Cervantes."[9] Geoffrey Stagg suggests that "Benengeli . . . , like the marabouts, though reputed 'sabio,' is to be charged with mendacity, fraud and deception."[10] And what happens if we do not make the distinction? If the reader identifies Cervantes with Cid Hamete in the latter's insensitivity, he must either cleave to the "author" and forsake the protagonist, in the manner of an Auerbach or perhaps even an Efron, or reject the author and embrace the protagonist in the manner of Unamuno, who is in fact an almost perfect model for the type of reader who refuses to make the distinction, because his refusal is thorough, wholehearted, and relentlessly pursued to its logical conclusions.[11]

9. "Three Versions of Don Quijote," p. 810.
10. "El sabio Cide Hamete Venengeli," p. 224.
11. Erich Auerbach, "The Enchanted Dulcinea," in *Mimesis: The Representation of Reality in Western Literature*, pp. 293–315; Arthur Efron, *Don Quixote and the Dulcineated World*; Miguel de Unamuno, *Vida de Don Quijote y Sancho*. Subsequent references in parentheses in the text are to Unamuno.

Let us consider briefly Unamuno's responses at some of the critical points in the alienation of the reader outlined above. On the reference to "childish bravado" in the episode of the lions: "Oh, damned Cid Hamete Benengeli, or whoever wrote this episode, how inadequately you understood it! It seems that Sansón Carrasco must have been whispering in your ear as you narrated it" (p. 132).

On the Cave of Montesinos: "On coming to this visionary adventure, the historian thinks himself obliged to doubt its authenticity! ... Oh, simple-minded historian, how little you understand about visionary experiences!" (p. 137).

On the characterization of Don Quixote and Sancho as "[two fools]": "Here the historian is as right as he can be, when he says that it is his personal opinion that the jesters were as crazy as their victims, and that the duke and duchess were not two fingers' breadth removed from being fools, when they went to so much trouble to make sport of two fools. . . . But stop right there, for neither Sancho nor Don Quixote can be called fools, and the duke and duchess can, because that's what they were" (p. 211).

Unamuno, who passes without comment over the transfer of the authorial mantle from Cervantes to Cid Hamete in I, IX, does not shrink from the inescapable consequences of the refusal to make a distinction: "Must we not consider that the greatest miracle accomplished by Don Quixote was his having had a man like Cervantes write the story of his life, a man who revealed in his other works the poverty of his genius, and how far he was, in the natural scheme of things, beneath what was required to narrate the deeds of the *Ingenioso Hidalgo* in the way in which he did, in fact, narrate them?" (p. 226). He rejects the "author" in order to embrace the protagonist. But Unamuno did not always feel this way about *Don Quixote*, and his earlier reaction to the novel illustrates the other possible consequence of the refusal to distinguish Cid Hamete's perspective from that of Cervantes— support of the author and rejection of the protagonist: "Some years ago, in a weekly of some authority and renown here in Spain, I shouted this war-cry: 'Death to Don Quixote!' . . . And today I confess to you, my lord, that that cry of mine was a cry

13

inspired in me by the one who vanquished you, Sansón Carrasco
..." (p. 197). Such unwillingness to dissociate Cervantes from Cid
Hamete is at the very heart of the remarkable polarity which has
characterized *Quixote* criticism for two hundred years. It has
also contributed significantly to the disproportionate difficulty
with which the "lay genius" position has been finally (?) discred-
ited.

The identification of Cid Hamete with Cervantes is fostered by
the final fusion of the two in the concluding paragraphs of the
novel when Cervantes remarks as follows: "Such was the end of
the Ingenious Gentleman of La Mancha, whose birthplace Cid
Hamete was unwilling to designate exactly..." (987). This recalls,
of course, the initial phrase, "In a village of La Mancha the name
of which I have no desire to recall " (25), which, as Riley points
out, must be ascribed to the implied Cervantes.[12] The final para-
graph begins with Cid Hamete addressing his pen, then quotes
the words which he puts in the mouth of the now personified pen:
"Hands off, o'erweening ones!/Let it by none attempted be
..."—words which are addressed to "presumptuous and scoun-
drelly historians." The pen is still speaking in the lines which
follow the ballad: "For me alone [*sola*] Don Quixote was born and
I for him" (988), but there is an almost imperceptible shift in
mid-sentence to Cervantes addressing the reader: "I shall be the
first one to enjoy the fruit of his own writings as fully as he
desired [*quedaré satisfecho*] ..." (988).

Now although Cervantes obliterates the distinction between
himself and Cid Hamete at the end of the novel, when the masks
are put away and the box of fiction closed, he does not thereby
invalidate the distinction nor imply a retroactive ratification of
the Moor's perspective on the characters and the events he
narrates. Cervantes never allows his own awareness of the subtle changes he has wrought in his protagonist to alter the
perspective of his obtuse and therefore unreliable narrator Cid
Hamete. It is true that he never suggests that he himself might
have a different perspective, except, ironically, before any difference has developed: "In this work, I am sure, will be found all that

12. Edward C. Riley, *Cervantes's Theory of the Novel*, p. 209.

14

could be desired in the way of pleasant reading; and if it is lacking in any way, I maintain that this is the fault of that hound of an author rather than of the subject" (73). But the whole complex structure of the novel leads the reader to increased identification with the protagonist and a corresponding estrangement from the narrator, and it is this structure that reveals Cervantes' own perspective.

If one is forced to choose between the assumption that Cervantes misunderstood the essential thrust of his own novel, as Cid Hamete's perspective seems to indicate, and the assumption that the two view the characters and events from different perspectives, can one but choose the latter?

2. THE GOVERNORSHIP OF SANCHO PANZA AND DON QUIXOTE'S CHIVALRIC CAREER

There is no such thing as luck in this world, and whatever happens, whether it be good or bad, does not occur by chance but through a special providence of Heaven.

Part II, Chapter LXVI

Much has been written of the reciprocal influence which Don Quixote and Sancho exert upon each other in the course of the novel, particularly since Salvador de Madariaga's seminal chapters on the Quixotization of Sancho and the Sanchification of Don Quixote in his *Don Quixote: An Introductory Essay in Psychology* (1961). But the structural, thematic, and stylistic correlation developed by Cervantes between Sancho's governorship and Don Quixote's chivalric career has not, to my knowledge, been delineated. Since such a correlation would constitute a significant factor in the ethical orientation of the reader, we should investigate more fully the parallels that have been observed between aspects of the governorship and the adventures of Don Quixote.

Leland Chambers has noted "Cervantes' parallel development of the dubbing of Don Quixote and the conferring of Sancho's governorship," and he concludes that since "both investitures become valid in spirit . . . the situations of both characters are essentially the same, and each accurately represents the world view of the novel."[1] Carlos Varo suggests the existence of a parallel between Sancho's self-discovery, a consequence of his experience as governor, and the fact that Don Quixote's ascent, in the reader's eyes, begins just when he ceases being a "mechanically optimistic" madman. Varo sees in the parallel an embodiment of Cervantes' belief in the redemptive capacity of suffering.[2] Joaquín Casalduero has pointed out that the "Cave of Montesinos, like the pit [into which Sancho falls after leaving Barataria] is an inward movement. . . . [Sancho] has known

1. "Structure and the Search for Truth in the *Quijote*," pp. 311–12.
2. *Génesis y evolución del "Quijote,"* p. 486n88.

19

disillusionment [*desengaño*], he has known himself. . . . Thanks to the fall into the pit he is able to purify himself of his desire to rule: 'Who would have said that he who yesterday was enthroned as the governor of an island . . . would today find himself buried in a pit? . . .'"[3] E. C. Riley has recently drawn attention to another facet of the same correspondence: "The parallel adventure [parallel to that of the Cave of Montesinos] of Sancho's fall into the pit is perhaps the only one in the book which gives the impression—at least such a strong impression—of having been introduced solely for symbolic reasons. Not that it is impossible, but it seems to be a fortuitous episode which is justified as a symbol of the fall of the 'mighty' from the pinnacle of Fortune, as a counterpart [*parangón*] to the Cave of Montesinos. . . ."[4] This last comment is particularly significant for its suggestion that Cervantes is especially concerned at this point to draw an analogy between the respective activities of the knight and his squire.

A parallel thus begins to emerge from the isolated comments of a number of critics, involving a change from the comic to the serious (Chambers), a fall (Riley), and the achievement of self-knowledge (Varo, Casalduero). I suggested in *Don Quixote: Hero or Fool?* (Part I, pp. 61–63) that in an important sense, the governorship of Sancho parallels in its principal outlines the genesis, practice, and renunciation of the chivalric mission of Don Quixote. I believe that Cervantes' treatment of the governorship, especially in its conclusion, is designed to elicit a rather clearly definable reaction from the reader, and that one's final perspective on the governorship informs one's reaction to both the chivalric career of Don Quixote and his renunciation at the end of the novel of what he had seen as his mission. This essay is an attempt to elucidate the parallels between Sancho's governorship and Don Quixote's career and to indicate what is being

3. *Sentido y forma del "Quijote,"* p. 343.
4. *"Don Quijote,"* in *Suma cervantina,* p. 71. Despite her assertion that the episode of Sancho's fall into the pit is to be understood in opposition to the episode of Don Quixote's descent into the Cave of Montesinos, Helena Percas de Ponseti notes that "his fall into the pit constitutes for him the revelation of his personal truth, as does Don Quixote's descent into the Cave of Montesinos for him, and it is constructed with analogous technical procedures" (*Cervantes y su concepto del arte,* pp. 630, 637).

foreshadowed in the treatment of the untimely end of the squire's brief moment of glory.

———•·•———

Don Quixote's initial goal is fame, to be obtained by imitating the heroes of the books of chivalry. We are told that the books he liked best were those of Feliciano de Silva, "whose lucid prose style and involved conceits were as precious to him as pearls" (26). The knight whom he most admired, at the outset, was "Rinaldo of Montalbán, especially as he beheld him sallying forth from his castle to rob all those that crossed his path. . ." (27). The initial attraction of the books of chivalry for Don Quixote, then, is esthetic, not ethical, and his desire to right wrongs is simply a necessary consequence of this attraction. Dulcinea is another consequence, and not a motivating force, and she is chosen, quite logically, after the more important business of Rocinante is attended to: "And so, having polished up his armor and made the morion over into a closed helmet, and having given himself and his horse a name, he naturally found but one thing lacking still: he must seek out a lady of whom he could become enamoured" (29). Of course, there is much subsequent talk of "righting wrongs," and this is the intent behind much of Don Quixote's activity because *that is what knights-errant do*, just as he spends a lot of time "thinking of his lady Dulcinea: *for this was in accordance with what he had read in his books. . .*" (65). But his tacit acceptance of the "chivalric" career of the innkeeper who knighted him ("he had done many wrongs, cheated many widows, ruined many maidens, and swindled not a few minors"), the determining factors in his choice of Amadís over Roland as a model (210–11), his elaboration of a knight's career (162–65), and his defense of the novels of chivalry in the argument with the canon (441–44) all manifest the primacy of the esthetic over the ethical.[5] It goes without saying that his initial esthetic percep-

5. See Juan Bautista Avalle-Arce's penetrating essay "Don Quijote o la vida como obra de arte": "Don Quijote confuses, purposely, undoubtedly, artistic imitation . . . with the emulation of conduct" (p. 348). See especially pp. 346–57.

tions and predilections are not only ludicrous, but diametrically opposed to Cervantes' own explicit insistence upon versimilitude and his desire to express himself in words that are "the proper ones, meaningful and well placed, expressive of your intention in setting them down and of what you wish to say, without any intricacy or obscurity" (15).

It seems equally clear that the initial attraction of the governorship for Sancho is the material gain to be had from it. He is willing to trade the governorship for the recipe for the balsam of Fierabras, which promises a quicker, easier, and perhaps larger financial return (77), and he wants his domain in Micomicón to be on the coast so that he can easily transport his black slaves to market (252, 270).

Don Quixote and Sancho begin their respective quests supremely self-confident. Each is characterized by that "serene unawareness" of inadequacy which D. C. Muecke proposes as a necessary attribute of the victim of situational irony.[6] At the outset of his adventures, Don Quixote "could already see himself crowned Emperor of Trebizond at the very least" (28). He expects to improve upon the exploits of his predecessors, for, as he says, if they rewarded their squires in their old age with "the title of count, or marquis at most, of some valley or province more or less ..., it well may be that within a week I shall win some kingdom with others dependent upon it, and it will be the easiest thing in the world to crown you king of one of them" (61–62). A similar self-confidence characterizes Sancho in the early chapters: "Your Grace should not forget that island you promised me; for no matter how big it is, I'll be able to govern it right enough" (61).

A closely related characteristic which the two share is a serious lack of self-knowledge, an extremely important element in the process under investigation since true self-knowledge is a prerequisite for the self-mastery that constitutes Don Quixote's victory in the end. "I know who I am" (49), he affirms, in the famous phrase so dear to Unamuno. He had thought, at this point, that he was Baldwin and that his neighbor was the Mar-

6. *Irony*, pp. 25–30.

quis of Mantua. Some chapters later he forgets Dulcinea altogether in elaborating imaginatively his rise to fame: "It only remains to find out what king of the Christians or the pagans is at war and has a beautiful daughter" (164). The king's daughter is to be his bride.

Sancho's lack of self-knowledge is beautifully represented in his reaction to the escalation of Don Quixote's ambitions for him from governor to king, referred to above:

> "In that case," said Sancho Panza, "if by one of those miracles of which your Grace was speaking I should become king, I would certainly send for Juana Gutiérrez, my old lady, to come and be my queen. . . ."
> "There is no doubt about it," Don Quixote assured him.
> "Well I doubt it," said Sancho, "for I think even if God were to rain kingdoms upon the earth, no crown would sit well on the head of Mari Gutiérrez, for I am telling you, sir, as a queen she is not worth two maravedis." (62)

As Lazarillo remarked, in a similar context: "How many people must there be in the world who flee from others because they don't see themselves as they really are!" The parallel between the knight and his squire is quite clear in this regard when each in turn ignores the unbridgeable chasm between his specific station in life and that to which he aspires. Don Quixote needs to be "of royal line or [at least] second cousin to an emperor" to marry the king's daughter. His actual situation is "a gentleman property-holder" (165). Sancho will be, as Don Quixote says, a count, and "in making you a count, I make a [nobleman] of you at the same time" (166). The squire feels he has the necessary background, "for there was a time in my life when I was the beadle of a confraternity." The terms of the two relationships are roughly proportionate: of royal line : a gentleman property-holder :: count : beadle.

The stylistic complement to this elaborate parallel preparation for Don Quixote's career and for Sancho's governorship can be seen most clearly in the mock-heroic passages dedicated to each at the outset of their respective undertakings. In the case of Don

Quixote, it is a mock-epic dawn description, which he himself has composed:

> No sooner had the rubicund Apollo spread over the face of the broad and spacious earth the gilded filaments of his beauteous locks, and no sooner had the little singing birds of painted plumage greeted with their sweet and mellifluous harmony the coming of the Dawn, who, leaving the soft couch of her jealous spouse, now showed herself to mortals at all the doors and balconies of the horizon that bounds La Mancha—no sooner had this happened than the famous knight, Don Quixote de la Mancha, forsaking his own downy bed and mounting his famous steed, Rocinante, fared forth and began riding over the ancient and famous Campo de Montiel. (31)

In the case of Sancho, it is a mock-epic invocation of Apollo:

> O perpetual discoverer of the antipodes, great taper of the world, eye of the heavens, sweet shaker of the water-coolers, Thymbraeus here, Phoebus there, archer in one place, in another a physician, father of poetry, inventor of music, thou who dost ever rise and, though appearing to do so, dost never set! 'Tis thee, O Sun, by whose aid man doth beget man, 'tis thee whom I beseech to favor and enlighten my darkened intellect that I may be able to give an absolutely exact account of the government of the great Sancho Panza. (797–98)[7]

Auerbach's characterization of *Don Quixote* as "a comedy in which well-founded reality holds madness up to ridicule,"[8] though inadequate as applied to the whole book, serves quite well to describe this first phase of the parallel trajectories of Don Quixote and Sancho. The *structure*, understood as the author's disposition of the constant elements of a fictional world (in Castro's terms, the "incitements" offered Don Quixote and Sancho by their world), the *plot* (i.e., the developmental arrangement of the characters' reactions to that world), and the *style* clearly lead

7. For a complementary discussion of these two passages in relation to other similar ones, see *Don Quixote: Hero or Fool?* (Part I), pp. 58–63.
8. Auerbach, *Mimesis*, p. 305.

24

the reader to expect a comic denouement for both characters: failure in the endeavor and reintegration with the world.

———•———

In seeking to identify the principal factors in the reversal of the reader's expectation of a comic denouement for Don Quixote's career and for the governorship of Sancho, I should perhaps begin by observing that although the dubbing of Don Quixote and the conferring of Sancho's governorship are widely separated in the novel, the fulfillment of the desires of both characters is achieved nearly simultaneously at the castle of the duke and duchess. The latter arrange for Don Quixote the first chivalric reception in his career, and "this was the first time that he really and wholly believed himself to be a true knight errant and not a fanciful one. . ." (709). The governorship of the "island" is conferred upon Sancho later the same day (718). Thus our attention is drawn to the analogy between their careers in preparation for the reversal.

Although considerable preparation for the reversal has already been accomplished, and thus the distance between reader and protagonist has already begun to diminish,[9] it is still possible for Cervantes to make the following comment, as Sancho sets out for the *ínsula*:

> And now, gentle reader, let the worthy Sancho go in peace and good luck go with him. You may expect two bushels of laughter when you hear how he deported himself in office. Meanwhile, listen to what happened to his master that same night, and if it does not make you laugh, it will at least cause you to part your lips in an apelike grin; for Don Quixote's adventures are to be greeted with astonishment [*admiración*] or with mirth. (790–91)

This piece of commentary might be seen as an explicit ratification by Cervantes of the conclusions I have drawn concerning the major thrust of the novel to this point, yet one wonders just

9. *Don Quixote: Hero or Fool?* (Part I), pp. 42–45.

how comfortable the reader is supposed to feel with that apelike grin on his face. As I have pointed out in chapter 1, there is just enough ambiguity in *admiración* to allow for the possibility that Cervantes has been working subtly in another direction for some time. How else are we to understand that Don Quixote's aid is now sought by Doña Rodríguez in utter seriousness, that Basilio and his friends took him home with them, "for they regarded him as a man of valor, with hair on his chest" (648), that, as Lester Crocker has observed, "Don Quixote embodies the great spiritual force of human aspirations, and Cervantes presents him as superior in moral fibre to the people who flout him,"[10] and that Sancho "ordered things so wisely that to this day his decrees are preserved in that town, under the title of *The Constitutions of the Great Governor, Sancho Panza*" (849)?

As I noted above, Cervantes develops comic expectations in the reader through three elements of characterization—flawed motivation, excessive self-confidence, and lack of self-knowledge—and an appropriate stylistic complement. Basic changes can be observed in all four respects as the novel progresses. The change in Don Quixote's motivation can perhaps best be seen in the ethical emphasis which he infuses into his originally esthetic drive for fame in imitation of the chivalric heroes, in Chapter VIII of Part II:

> In confronting giants, it is the sin of pride that we slay, even as we combat envy with generosity and goodness of heart; anger, with equanimity and a calm bearing; gluttony and an overfondness for sleep, by eating little when we do eat and by keeping long vigils; lust and lewdness, with the loyalty that we show to those whom we have made the mistresses of our affections; and sloth, by going everywhere in the world in search of opportunities that may and do make of us famous knights as well as better Christians. You behold here, Sancho, the means by which one may attain the highest praise that the right sort of fame brings with it. (559)

It is significant that of these six of the seven Deadly Sins

10. *"Don Quijote*, Epic of Frustration," p. 180.

26

—avarice is missing—the only one which is not yet de-mythologized, that is, which Don Quixote still sees as external, is *la soberbia*; pride is in fact Don Quixote's nemesis.

As for Sancho, though he can still tell Teresa, who always brings out his most materialistic tendencies, that "in a few days from now I will be setting out for my government, where I go with a great desire to make money" (750), the attitude which more properly characterizes his actual selfless performance in the governorship is best expressed in conversation with Don Quixote:

> Let the island come, and I'll do my best to be such a gover-nor that, in spite of all the rascals, I'll go straight to Heaven. It's not out of greed that I want to quit my humble station or better myself; it is because I wish to see what it's like to be a governor." (779)

In dealing with the intrusions of self-doubt and the acquisition of self-knowledge during the phase of performance which I am just now attempting to characterize, it is difficult not to antici-pate, for the process only comes to fruition in confession and repentance at the point of anagnorisis, with which we are not yet concerned. In the case of Don Quixote, perhaps it is enough to note that the self-confident "I am worth a hundred" of Chapter XV, Part I, becomes: "This world is nothing but schemes and plots, all working at cross-purposes. I can do no more," in Chapter XXIX, Part II (703), before being definitively transcended in Don Quixote's reflection after his second encounter with Sansón Ca-rrasco: "Each man is the architect of his own fortune. I was the architect of mine, but I did not observe the necessary prudence, and as a result my presumptuousness has brought me to a sorry end" (943).

Similarly, the "I know who I am, and who I may be, if I choose" of Chapter V, Part I, becomes: "Up to now, I do not know what I have won with all the hardships I have endured. However, if my lady Dulcinea were but free of those that she is suffering, it may be that my fortunes would improve, and with a sounder mind I should be able to tread a better path than the one I follow at

27

present," in Chapter LVIII of Part II (884), before culminating in the final pages of the novel: "I am no longer Don Quixote de la Mancha but Alonso Quijano, whose mode of life won for him the name of 'Good'" (984).

As for Sancho, just before he takes office, he is able to say to Don Quixote:

> If your Grace is of the opinion that I am not fitted for this governorship, I give it up here and now; for I am more concerned for the black-of-the-nail of my soul than for my entire body. . . . I know no more about governing islands than a buzzard does, and if I thought for a minute that in order to be a governor the devil would have to carry me off, then I would rather go to Heaven as Sancho than go to Hell as governor. (787–88)

This element of self-doubt is accompanied by an increased measure of self-knowledge, for he tells the duke: "Let them clothe me any way they like, for however I go dressed, I'll still be Sancho Panza" (779), and he is quick to point out to the majordomo in Barataria that "there has never been any 'Don' in my family. Plain Sancho Panza they call me . . ." (798).

As Sancho overcomes his desire for material gain, he judges wisely, out of a credible combination of peasant shrewdness, memories from folk traditions, and the advice of Don Quixote. As Don Quixote shifts his emphasis from reliance upon the strength of his arm to the cultivation of strength of spirit, as he internalizes the struggle and demythologizes the giants of pride, Cervantes shows him victorious simply by virtue of the attempt (the episode of the lions, Clavileño), and finally victor even in defeat at the hands of the Knight of the White Moon—"victor over himself" (978).

The phase of the careers which we are now examining is characterized by surprisingly laudable performance accompanied by a shift in motivation, a loss of unwarranted confidence, and a deeper knowledge of self. If the madness of desire distorts one's perception of reality (particularly of one's self), achievement of the ostensible goal apparently sharpens one's perception of reality. Sancho is purified of his greed as Don Quixote is purged of his egocentric blindness and presumption. Both transcend narrow, undisciplined self-interest.

Before discussing the stylistic component in the reversal of comic expectations and preparation for a serious denouement, it is necessary to focus briefly upon two major thematic parallels which arise as consequences of the surprisingly laudable performance of both Don Quixote and Sancho—*el cuerdo-loco* and *los burladores burlados*—and to examine the crucial episode of the Cave of Montesinos and its parallels in Sancho's experience. The characterization of Don Quixote as *cuerdo-loco* is a central element in the extended encounter with Don Diego de Miranda. The latter vacillates continually in his appraisal of the knight, who "impressed him as being a crazy sane man and an insane one on the verge of sanity" (618). In subsequent chapters the madness of Don Quixote recedes at times to such an extent that it entirely escapes the notice of those he meets, even that of such a clever man as Basilio, who spends three days with Don Quixote after the wedding. The corresponding theme in Sancho's career as governor is that of the *discreto-tonto*. After Sancho had made a series of perspicacious judgments, the man whose duty it was to record his activities for the duke "could not make up his mind as to whether he should take the new governor for a fool or set him down as a wise man" (801), and by the time he left Barataria, he left everyone "filled with admiration at the words he had spoken and at the firmness and wisdom of his resolve" (860). The Sancho "with very few wits in his head" of Chapter VII, Part I (60) and the Don Quixote of Chapter I, "his wits . . . gone beyond repair" (27), have clearly run a parallel course, and if in Chapter II of Part II the curate speaks of "the madness of the master [and] the foolishness of the man" (522), by the end of the novel it is possible for someone to say: "If the man is as wise as that, what must the master be!" (945).

The theme of *los burladores burlados* develops similarly in Part II. Don Quixote initiates the process with his defeat of Sansón Carrasco in Chapter XIV, frustrating the latter's plans to force him to remain at home for two years. As Tomé Cecial remarks to

Sansón: "Don Quixote is a madman and we are sane, yet he goes away sound and laughing while your Grace is left here, battered and sorrowful" (601). Most of the manifestations of the theme, however, are more the work of the author than of Don Quixote himself: the duke is nonplussed when Doña Rodríguez seeks Don Quixote's aid in resolving a problem which the duke, to his discredit, is unwilling to deal with (821); she reveals to Don Quixote the intimate defects of both the duchess and Altisidora (822); the duke is chagrined when Tosilos concedes the battle with Don Quixote (876); finally, Altisidora angrily drops the pose of lovesick damsel, stung by the knight's consistent refusal to succumb to her attempted seduction (966).

In the parallel phase of Sancho's governorship, the point is explicitly made by the majordomo:

> I am indeed astonished to hear a man wholly unlettered, as I believe your Grace to be, uttering so many wise maxims and observations, all of which is quite contrary to what was expected of your Grace's intelligence by those who sent us and by us who came here with you. Each day new things are seen in this world, jests are turned into earnest and the jesters are mocked. (825)

Almost all of the material discussed in this phase of the reversal of comic expectations for both Don Quixote and Sancho is drawn from the period of their sojourn with the duke and duchess, the pinnacle of worldly achievement for both; but a crucial episode for Don Quixote—the Cave of Montesinos—precedes their arrival at the castle, and Cervantes draws subtle but explicit parallels in the experience of Sancho, one before and one after his governorship.

The *topos* which informs the episode of the Cave of Montesinos is a classic one. The motif is the hero's descent into the underworld, and the theme is the hero's search for wisdom.[11] The adventure is appropriately a dream, an occasionally grotesque amalgam of recent experience, fears, and aspirations, and thus a revealing descent into the protagonist's unconscious. His report

11. Robert Scholes and Robert Kellogg, *The Nature of Narrative*, p. 27.

of the dream (which neither he nor Cid Hamete recognize as such) reveals a mind in precarious balance between the pretensions and aspirations with which he began, as reflected in Montesinos' reception and his presentation of the knight to Durandarte, and a dawning sense of inadequacy, as reflected in both Durandarte's reaction ("patience, and shuffle") and Dulcinea's request for a loan, illuminated for us by Gerald Brenan.[12] The outward manifestations of these two poles are represented most clearly in Don Quixote's reckless valor in the adventure of the lions (II, XVI) and in his fearful flight in the episode of the braying aldermen (II, XXVII). His sense of inadequacy will not be consciously articulated until immediately after he leaves the duke's castle, in his reflections upon encountering the images of the saints (884).

There is a double parallel in Sancho's experience. Sancho's account of the ride on Clavileño is the comic counterpart of the pretensions of his master in the cave, and it is Don Quixote himself who explicitly points up the analogy in a desperate bid for support in his flagging attempts to keep the faith: "Sancho, if you want us to believe what you saw in Heaven, then you must believe me when I tell you what I saw in the Cave of Montesinos. I need say no more" (778). The squire's fall into the pit corresponds to the dark side of his master's vision in the cave. Sancho, quite naturally, is struck by the difference between the two subterranean adventures:

> I'll not be as lucky as was my master, Señor Don Quixote de la Mancha, when he went down into the cave of that enchanted Montesinos, where he came upon people who entertained him better than if he had been in his own house. Why, it seems as if they had the table already laid for him and the bed made; he saw beautiful and pleasant visions there, but all that I'll see here will be toads and snakes. (868)

But his view of the place of the event in his recent experience both harks back to the intimations of inadequacy in Don Qui-

12. *The Literature of the Spanish People*, pp. 185–90.

31

xote's dream and points toward his master's final realization of his own error:

> Who would ever have said that he who yesterday was enthroned as the governor of an island . . . would today find himself buried in a pit? . . . Where have my follies and my fancies brought me? (868)

This adventure is a "symbol of the fall of the 'mighty' from the pinnacle of Fortune, as a counterpart to the Cave of Montesinos . . . ," as E. C. Riley observes, and, we must add, a foreshadowing and portent of the fall of Don Quixote, who must also one day admit his errors: "My presumptuousness has brought me to a sorry end" (943), "I realize how foolish I was . . ." (984). But the serious business of confession and repentance which constitutes the final stage of the process of *desengaño* requires an appropriate stylistic complement, one radically different from the mock-heroic style with which the two parallel trajectories began.

Sancho is of course the first to fall, and the narrator's commentary in preparation for the account of the end of the governorship adopts a tone which is heard for the first time in the novel:

> To imagine that things in this life are always to remain as they are is to indulge in an idle dream. It would appear, rather, that everything moves in a circle, that is to say, around and around: spring follows summer, summer the harvest season, harvest autumn, autumn winter, and winter spring; and thus does time continue to turn like a never-ceasing wheel. Human life alone hastens onward to its end, swifter than time's self and without hope of renewal, unless it be in that other life that has no bounds. So sayeth Cid Hamete, the Mohammedan philosopher; for many who have lacked the light of faith, being guided solely by the illumination that nature affords them, have yet attained to a comprehension of the swiftness and instability of this

present existence and the eternal duration of the one we hope for. Our author, however, is here thinking of the speed with which Sancho's government was overthrown and brought to a close, and, so to speak, sent up in smoke and shadow. (855–56)

As I have pointed out before, "the subject is no longer 'the government of the *great* Sancho Panza,' and, though there is humor in the passage ('that is to say, around and around'; 'the Mohammedan philosopher'), it is not directed at Sancho." Further, "the seriousness of the analogy (death : governorship) and the level of style contrast with the mock-epic invocation" that introduced the governorship.[13] There is only one other passage in the novel like this one in tone and content—the preparation for the end of Don Quixote's career and for his death:

Inasmuch as nothing that is human is eternal but is ever declining from its beginning to its close, this being especially true of the lives of men, and since Don Quixote was not endowed by Heaven with the privilege of staying the downward course of things, his own end came when he was least expecting it. (983)

These passages introduce the moment of maximum lucidity, of disillusionment, for both characters. Sancho has been defeated, and now he sees clearly: "Since leaving you and mounting the towers of ambition and pride, a thousand troubles, a thousand torments, and four thousand worries have entered my soul. . . . I was not born to be a governor. . . . In this stable I leave behind me the ant's wings that lifted me in the air so that the swifts and other birds might eat me" (858–59). "'And what did you get out of your government?' asked Ricote. 'I got the knowledge that I am not fit to govern anything, unless it be a herd of cattle'" (865).

Don Quixote experiences a parallel recognition. "My mind now is clear, unencumbered by those misty shadows of ignorance.

13. *Don Quixote: Hero or Fool?* (Part I), p. 62.

33

. . . I am no longer Don Quixote de la Mancha . . ." (984). His islanders may exhort Sancho to get up and celebrate his "victory" over the invaders, Sansón may remind Don Quixote that Dulcinea is now disenchanted, and Sancho himself may implore his master not to "let himself die," to blame him for his defeat, but each of them, in his own critical moment of recognition, *knows* the truth.

Failure lays bare the internal inadequacy and gives rise to definitive self-knowledge, humility, and confession, which issue in what the seventeenth-century Spaniard called *desengaño*.

———————•———————

Both Sancho and Don Quixote, then, have lived through a process beginning with pride and presumption and a consequent unawareness of their limitations, moving toward self-discovery through suffering, and culminating in confession and repentance. Both of them say this explicitly. Their experiences have not befallen them by chance, and here one must be careful not to draw the wrong conclusions from E. C. Riley's allusion to the "fall of the 'mighty' from the pinnacle of Fortune." "There is no such thing as [fortune] in this world, and whatever happens, whether it be good or bad, does not occur by chance but through a special providence of Heaven . . . ," says the enlightened Don Quixote (*943) in almost the same words as Cervantes in the *Persiles*: "That which is commonly called Fortune . . . is nothing other than a firm disposition of Heaven."[14]

Recognition, confession, and repentance are ratified in epiphany. As Don Quixote and Sancho approach the end of the third and final sally,

> they [mount] a slope from the top of which they [have] a
> view of their village, at the sight of which Sancho [falls] on
> his knees.
> "Open your eyes, O beloved homeland," he [cries], "and

14. *Los trabajos de Persiles y Sigismunda*, vol. 2, ed. R. Schevill and A. Bonilla (Madrid: B. Rodríguez, 1914), p. 291.

behold your son, Sancho Panza, returning to you. If he does not come back very rich, he comes well flogged. Open your arms and receive also your other son, Don Quixote, who returns vanquished by the arm of another but a victor over himself; and this, so I have been told, is the greatest victory that could be desired. . . . "(977–78)

At the end of a similarly long and arduous journey, Persiles and Sigismunda finally approach their goal, Rome, about to reassume their own original identities: "The other pilgrims in our company, coming in sight of Rome, from a hill looked down upon it, and falling on their knees, they adored it as a holy place" (II, 221). Alban Forcione has indicated the significance of this ritualistic ascension: "As Frye points out, the hill is one of the archetypal locations for the point of epiphany, at which the 'undisplaced apocalyptic world and the cyclical world of nature come into alignment.' Like the Bible, the *Persiles* presents several mountain-top epiphanies. . . ."[15]

The epiphany does not include Sancho; on the contrary, though it is he who articulates the statement which makes explicit the implicit process of self-mastery as victory, his own situation represents a comic reduction of Don Quixote's self-discovery since he is unable to assimilate fully the lessons of the governorship. It is precisely the bogus lashings alluded to in the epiphany scene which constitute the sign of Sancho's backsliding into greed and thus of his inability to follow his master on the plane of transcendence. His is a comic reintegration into the world such as the reader was initially led to expect, and the common view of Sancho as Don Quixote's disciple at the end of the novel, ready to carry forward his master's quixotic quest, is simply incompatible with the text. It would nevertheless be ill advised to judge Sancho too harshly, for he survives his moment of recognition. One cannot live in the rarefied atmosphere of

15. *Cervantes' Christian Romance: A Study of "Persiles y Sigismunda,"* pp. 35–36. The quotation from Northrup Frye is from *Anatomy of Criticism* (Princeton: Princeton University Press, 1957), p. 203.

transcendence, for to live is to err. Which is why Don Quixote must die at the moment of maximum lucidity.

> Here lies a gentleman bold
> Who was so very brave
> He went to lengths untold,
> And on the brink of the grave
> Death had on him no hold.
>
> By the world he set small store—
> He frightened it to the core—
> Yet somehow, by Fate's plan,
> Though he'd lived a crazy man,
> When he died he was sane once more.

3. STRATEGIES OF IRONY
IN "DON QUIXOTE"

Is Cervantes joking? And what is he making
fun of?

José Ortega y Gasset,
Meditaciones del "Quijote"

To attempt to investigate systematically the targets, the limits, and the relative stability or instability of the irony in *Don Quixote* and its deployment in the service of the norms which govern life in the world of Cervantes' masterpiece is a quixotic endeavor. It involves two hopelessly complex phenomena—irony and *Don Quixote*—and one is led inescapably into the kind of moral and ethical discriminations which contemporary criticism has so judiciously sought to avoid. One must ask, nevertheless, what else is to be done with the "camp of Agramante" of *Quixote* criticism, where the "partisans of the helmet," the "partisans of the basin," and the "partisans of the basin-helmet" continue to press with ever increasing ingenuity their respective claims concerning the true meaning of the novel?[1]

The discovery by the Romantics of unsuspected depths in *Don Quixote* must be seen, finally, as having been purchased too dear. That is the significance of recent studies such as those of Russell and Close. The perspectivist critics, insofar as they have really kept the faith, have exulted in the unlimited possibilities of the reconstruction of meanings (e.g., Percas), and the ideologues have constructed elaborate, mutually exclusive edifices in which scarcely one stone of the original structure is left upon another (Unamuno, Efron).[2]

1. These designations of the rival camps of *Quixote* critics appear in Cesáreo Bandera, *Mimesis conflictiva*, p. 155. The partisans of the helmet, partisans of the basin, and partisans of the basin-helmet are, respectively, the "soft," "hard," and "perspectivist" schools, well known in Cervantes criticism and defined in *Don Quixote: Hero or Fool?* (Part I), pp. 3–6.

2. P. E. Russell, "*Don Quixote* as a Funny Book"; Anthony J. Close, "*Don Quixote* and the 'Intentionalist Fallacy,'" "Sancho Panza: Wise Fool," "Don Qui-

The consideration of three sets of questions is central to any resolution, individual or collective, of the impasse at which critical discussion of *Don Quixote* has arrived: (1) Who are the victims and what are the objects or targets of Cervantes' irony? Is there in fact more there than the early readers seem to have seen? (2) Are there discernible indications as to where to stop in ironic reconstruction, indications that clearly preclude the possibility of further rationally defensible exegetical constructions? In other words, is the irony *limited*? (3) Can we identify the norms implicit in the ironies sufficiently to adumbrate the strategies behind them? In other words, is the irony *stable*?

I see no way to support answers to these vexing questions without a painstaking examination, first, of the Prologue and the first sally of the *Quixote* of 1605. If, after such an exercise, we readers continue to differ in our responses to the text, as we will, we shall at least be able to see more precisely where and perhaps why this is so. And if we can establish the identity of the targets and the limits of the scope of the irony in the initial stages of *Don Quixote*, we can go on to the rest of the novel better prepared to spot the subsequent changes of targets or scope which would necessarily characterize a shift in Cervantes' strategies of irony.

The reader may note the infrequency of references in the body of this chapter to the many statements about and investigations of irony in *Don Quixote*. Most discussions of irony in Cervantes' novel are either quite general, and heavily involved with Romantic "paradoxical" irony, or very specific and very limited. They are therefore of little help in the attempt to specify the rhetoric which justifies calling a particular passage ironic. Percas' perspectivist view that irony is, like beauty, in the eye of the beholder implies an entirely different focus.[3] Castro is very

---

xote's Love for Dulcinea," "Don Quixote as a Burlesque Hero," and *The Romantic Approach to "Don Quixote"*; Helena Percas de Ponseti, *Cervantes y su concepto del arte*; Miguel de Unamuno, *Vida de don Quijote y Sancho*; Arthur Efron, *Don Quixote and the Dulcineated World*.

3. "If in the *Quixote* of 1605 the irony, bordering at times on parody and sarcasm, gave us some indication of the thought of the author, in the *Quixote* of 1615 the irony depends, more frequently, upon the point of reference of the reader, upon the theme which he conceives of as central in each episode and of the focus which he brings to the reading": *Cervantes y su concepto del arte*, p. 648.

suggestive, but not very helpful when it comes to specifics. A statement such as: "ultraexpressivity, accumulation of words, usually points to double or oblique meaning (irony or defensive caution)"[4] is, in effect, tautological since the perception of irony is what leads the reader to find that the "expressivity" is "ultra–." Murillo's interest is in the ironies that he perceives in the relationship between *Don Quixote* and Cervantes' life. Hatzfeld's study is extensive and specific, but focused upon the stylistic variety exemplified by series of what are, for my purposes, undifferentiated examples.[5] Close's articles (cited above) dealing with irony in *Don Quixote* are, on the other hand, extremely perceptive and useful, and not, I think, at all incompatible with the conclusions of this study as far as he goes in his citations from the novel, which is, essentially, as far as the sojourn with the duke and duchess.

A common approach is to set the text against one's interpretation of it and then identify as ironic those passages which run counter to the interpretation. Thus, for example, for Efron, "peace is the true end of war" is ironic; for Castro, the presentation of Don Diego de Miranda is ironic, and so forth.[6] Since my investigation in this chapter supports my interpretation of the novel, I am, of course, open to the same charge. The only rational defense against it seems to me to lie in the attempt to assume responsibility for a *comprehensive* treatment of irony in *Don Quixote*, to specify the rhetorical justification in each instance, and to indicate the mutual relationships and overall coherence of the strategies in the service of which the tactics of individual instances are employed.

I have dispensed with a preliminary discussion of irony and an exposition of the classifications and definitions I will use here in

4. Américo Castro, *Hacia Cervantes*, p. 370n.
5. L. A. Murillo, "Cervantic Irony: The Problem for Literary Criticism," in *Homenaje a Rodríguez Moñino*, 2:21–27; Helmut Hatzfeld, *El "Quijote" como obra de arte del lenguaje*, pp. 153–206, esp. pp. 185–94. As a test of the representativeness of my examples, the reader may wish to compare Hatzfeld's examples of "ironía formal" (pp. 185–87), which I deliberately examined only after completing this study, with those adduced here.
6. Efron, *Don Quixote and the Dulcineated World*, p. 111; Castro, "Como veo ahora el *Quijote*," in *El ingenioso hidalgo don Quijote de la Mancha*, pp. 90–99.

the hope that these matters will be clearer if they are allowed to surface in connection with specific examples, conclusions, and summaries as these arise. I am encouraged in that hope by the observation that the theorists of irony to whom I refer throughout the following analysis must themselves have recourse to series of illustrative examples every step of the way.

I. THE PROLOGUE AND THE FIRST SALLY

The Prologue

1.   Idling reader, you may believe me [without my swearing to it] when I tell you that I should have liked this book, which is the child of my brain, to be the fairest, the sprightliest, and the cleverest that could be imagined; (*11)

The potential irony of the implicit contrast between "without my swearing to it" and "I swear that" (tacitly rejected) does not survive the realization that the rest of the sentence can only be taken at face value.

2.   but I have not been able to contravene the law of nature which would have it that like begets like. And so, what was to be expected of *a sterile and uncultivated wit* such as that which I possess if not [the story of] an offspring that was dried up, shriveled, and eccentric, a story filled with thoughts that never occurred to anyone else,

The reader immediately recognizes the conventional ironic self-deprecation for which his experience of prologues has prepared him (e.g., Lázaro: "this trifle which I have written in this vulgar style"). Among the attributes of the as-yet-unnamed Don Quixote, he may notice Cervantes' covert claim to originality in "thoughts that never occurred to anyone else."

3.   of a sort that might be engendered in a prison where every annoyance has its home and every mournful sound its habitation? Peace and tranquillity, the pleasures of

the countryside, the serenity of the heavens, the murmur of fountains, and ease of mind can do much toward causing the most unproductive of muses to become fecund and bring forth progeny that will be the marvel and delight of mankind.

The reader may be unsure whether the allusion to the prison is to be taken literally or not, but neither interpretation affects the direction in which he is being led.

4.   It sometimes happens that a father has an ugly son with no redeeming grace whatever, yet love will draw a veil over the parental eyes which then behold only cleverness and beauty in place of defects, and in speaking to his friends, he will make those defects out to be the signs of comeliness and intellect. I, however, who, [although I seem to be his father], am but Don Quixote's stepfather, have no desire to go with the current of custom,

The metaphor which builds from the first sentence (the book as "the child of my brain"), through the statement that the author has engendered the story of a son, to the contrast between those fathers who are blind to their children's faults and the author, who chooses to be different, may seem skewed by the clause "although I seem to be his father, I am but Don Quixote's stepfather." It is the reader who has gone astray, however, for the consistent logic of the sequence is that Cervantes "fathered" the book, but not the protagonist. The possible meaning of "stepfather" is at this point unknown.

5.   nor would I, *dearest reader*, beseech you with tears in my eyes as others do to pardon or overlook the faults you discover in this book; you are neither relative nor friend but may call your soul your own and exercise your free judgment. You are in your own house where you are master as the king is of his taxes, for you are familiar with the saying, "Under my cloak I kill the king." All of which exempts and frees you from any kind of respect or obligation; you may say of this story whatever you choose without fear of being slandered for an ill opinion any more than you will be rewarded for a good one.

43

The continuation of the passage completes the conventional pattern initiated earlier of authorial self-deprecation and praise/placation of the reader. The reader may or may not sense the irony of "dearest reader," which clearly moves in a direction opposite to "nor would I . . . beseech you." But this makes no particular difference since the combined effect is still that of placation of the reader, though at different levels of sophistication.

6.   I should like to bring you the tale unadulterated and unadorned, stripped of the usual prologue and the endless string of sonnets, epigrams, and eulogies such as are commonly found at the beginning of books. For I may tell you that, although I expended no little labor upon the work itself, I have found no task more difficult than the composition of this preface which you are now reading. Many times I took up my pen and many times I laid it down again, not knowing what to write.

The satiric possibility introduced earlier with "I . . . have no desire to go with the current of custom," as yet undeveloped, is reasserted here with "the endless string of sonnets, epigrams, and eulogies such as are commonly found at the beginning of books." The reader is led to differentiate the author's attitude toward prologues from his attitude toward conventional prefatory poems (devalued by "endless string") because of the seriousness with which he seems to regard the one that the reader is reading.

7.   On one occasion when I was thus in suspense, paper before me, pen over my ear, elbow on the table, and chin in hand, a very clever friend of mine came in. Seeing me lost in thought, he inquired as to the reason, and I made no effort to conceal from him the fact that my mind was on the preface which I had to write for the story of Don Quixote, and that it was giving me so much trouble that I had about decided not to write any at all and to abandon entirely the idea of publishing the exploits of so noble a knight.

"How," I said to him, "can you expect me not to be

concerned over what that venerable legislator, the Public, will say when it sees me, at my age, after all those years of silent slumber, coming out with *a tale that is as dried as a rush, a stranger to invention, paltry in style, impoverished in content, and wholly lacking in learning and wisdom,*

The reader must interpret the passage up to this point as a continuation of the conventional authorial self-deprecation with which the Prologue began.

8.   without marginal citations or notes at the end of the book when other works of this sort, even though they be fabulous and profane, are so packed with maxims from Aristotle and Plato and the whole crowd of philosophers as to *fill the reader with admiration and lead him to regard the author as a well read, learned, and eloquent individual?*

The abrupt shift from a list of truly desirable qualities which the author pretends are lacking in his book, to the undesirable apparatus of pseudoscholarship which now becomes the target of satire, is signaled by the reservation "though they be fabulous and profane" and by the pejorative "crowd" (*caterva*). One could argue that the satiric erosion retroactively undermines "impoverished in content and wholly lacking in learning and wisdom" without affecting the movement or direction of the thrust.

9.   Not to speak of the citations from Holy writ! *You would think they were at the very least so many St. Thomases and other doctors of the Church;*

The satiric reduction by means of hyperbolic praise is sharpened by the postulation of a multiplicity of rivals of Aquinas, the conventional unique exemplar.

10.   for *they [observe decorum so ingeniously* that], having portrayed in one line a distracted lover, in the next they will give *a nice little Christian sermon that is a joy and a privilege to hear and to read.*

The reader can scarcely fail to perceive the satire involved in the

45

invocation of a standard esthetic principle in praise of an example of its flagrant violation. The diminutive "nice little . . . sermon" suggests the inconsequential, hypocritical introduction of a "moral."

11. "All this my book will lack, for I have no citations for the margins, no notes for the end. To tell the truth, I do not even know who the authors are to whom I am indebted, and so am unable to follow the example of all the others by listing them alphabetically at the beginning, starting with Aristotle and closing with Xenophon, or, perhaps, with Zoilus or Zeuxis, notwithstanding the fact that the former was a snarling critic, the latter a painter.

Here the reader is given another signal in the pattern of "though they be fabulous and profane" which identifies the impropriety of the practice satirized.

12. This work will also be found lacking in prefatory sonnets by dukes, marquises, counts, bishops, ladies, and poets of great renown; although if I were to ask two or three [artisan friends] of mine, they would supply the deficiency by furnishing me with productions that could not be equaled by the authors of most repute in all Spain.

Despite the deflation achieved by (1) lumping the poetry of famous poets with that of "dukes, marquises, counts, bishops, ladies," and (2) the comment that two or three artisans could write better poetry than that exemplified in the prefatory verse written by the most famous contemporary Spanish poets, this passage affects neither the range nor the targets of the satire.

13. "In short, my friend," I went on, "I am resolved that Señor Don Quixote shall remain buried in the archives of La Mancha until Heaven shall provide him with someone to deck him out with all the ornaments that he lacks;

At this point the reader may resolve the uncertainty which as yet surrounds the meaning of "stepfather": the author is a historian.

46

14. for *I find myself incapable* of remedying the situation, *being possessed of little learning or aptitude*, and *I am, moreover, extremely lazy* when it comes to hunting up authors who will say for me what I [know how to say without them]. And if I am in a state of suspense and my thoughts are woolgathering, you will find a sufficient explanation in what I have just told you."

The self-deprecation continued here with "incapable," "little learning or aptitude," and "lazy" is now not only explicitly exposed as an ironic pose, but is in fact replaced by a bald assertion of self-sufficiency. The reader infers that the genuine hesitance which Cervantes seems to feel about publishing *Don Quixote* (reflected in the reference to his age and of the twenty years elapsed since the appearance of *La Galatea*, his last-published work) is due more to doubts about the reception of his new book than to a lack of confidence in his own capacity. The reader may perceive irony in the phrase "lazy when it comes to hunting up authors who will say for me what I [know how to say without them]" at another level if he is aware that Cervantes cribbed most of the Dedication which precedes the Prologue from Herrera (*Poesías de Garcilaso*, 1580).

15. Hearing this, my friend struck his forehead with the palm of his hand and burst into a loud laugh.

   "In the name of God, brother," he said, "you have just deprived me of an illusion. . . ."

   "Tell me, then," I replied, "how you propose to [fill the void of my fear and reduce to clarity the chaos of my confusion]?"

The style of the author's reply prepares the reader for the ironic advice now to be offered by the friend. The hyperbole and the elaborate parallel construction

and $\begin{cases} \text{"fill} & \text{the void} & \text{of my fear} \\ \text{reduce to clarity} & \text{the chaos} & \text{of my confusion"} \end{cases}$

clearly overdramatize the situation.

47

16.

The irony of the advice that follows (that Cervantes should invent poems and authors, insert unnecessary citations to support platitudes, bring up names simply in order to cite authoritative sources, append a list of authors without regard to whether or not they have been read or referred to) is easily identified through *the explicit advocacy of lying, the transparent cynicism* ("even though they make you out to be a liar, they are not going to cut off the hand that put these things on paper"; "what if the imposition is plain for all to see? You have little need to refer to them, and so it does not matter"; "no one is going to put himself to the trouble of verifying your references"), *the base purposes of the activity recommended* ("you can cause yourself to be taken for a grammarian"; "an allusion that will do you great credit"; "this imposing list of authors will at least give your book an unlooked-for air of authority"), and *the minimal effort to be expended and the cavalier attitude to be taken* ("you can remedy that by taking a little trouble"; "those scraps of Latin that you know by heart"; "which you can do by putting yourself out very little"; "one allusion which costs you little or nothing").

17.   "This is especially true in view of the fact that your book stands in no need of all these things whose absence you lament; for the entire work is an attack upon the books of chivalry of which Aristotle never dreamed. . . . You have no sermon to preach to anyone by mingling the human with the divine, a kind of motley in which no Christian intellect should be willing to clothe itself.

In the course of reading this passage one sees that the friend, who is, after all, the "author" of all the clues listed above and hence is recognized as a conscious ironist in what has preceded, has now put irony aside in preparation for the serious advice which is to follow. That the statement of the purpose of Cervantes' book ("the entire work is an attack upon the books of chivalry") marks the turning point is seen in retrospect when one reaches the judgment on mixing "the human with the divine," which neatly opposes the ironic praise by Cervantes earlier of the

48

"decorum so ingeniously" observed in the juxtaposition of "a distracted lover" and "a nice little Christian sermon." The statement of purpose acquires solid authority when it is reiterated in the passage that follows—a context of esthetic principles the seriousness of which is made clear by contrast with the elements previously satirized—and when it is restated again by the friend in closing:

18.   "All that you have to do is to make proper use of imitation in what you write, and the more perfect the imitation the better will your writing be. Inasmuch as you have no other object in view than that of overthrowing the authority and prestige which books of chivalry enjoy in the world at large and among the vulgar, there is no reason why you should go begging maxims of the philosophers, counsels of Holy Writ, fables of the poets, orations of the rhetoricians, or miracles of the saints; see to it, rather, that your style flows along smoothly, pleasingly, and sonorously, and that your words are the proper ones, meaningful and well placed, expressive of your intention in setting them down and of what you wish to say, without any intricacy or obscurity.
      "Let it be your aim that, by reading your story, the melancholy may be moved to laughter and the cheerful man made merrier still; let the simple not be bored, but may the clever admire your originality; let the grave ones not despise you, but let the prudent praise you. And keep in mind, above all, your purpose, which is that of undermining the ill-founded edifice that is constituted by those books of chivalry, so abhorred by many but admired by many more; if you succeed in attaining it, you will have accomplished no little." (15)

The opposition between the literary vices satirized and the esthetic principles exalted in the Prologue is clear: mediocre prefatory verse, false erudition, pedantry, and the mixture of erotic subject matter and religious sermonizing are *bad*, and straightforward, clear, decorous, unpretentious narrative informed by a consistent overall purpose is *good*. Vanity, hypocrisy, and carelessness are opposed to modesty, sincerity, and craftsmanship.

49

There is no ambiguity in the Prologue. The reader is not led to feel superior to some other, hypothetical, less perceptive reader who would miss the clues to the presence, targets, and limits of the irony, except as the satiric thrusts may be directed at one or another specific individual (Lope, Antonio de Guevara, "Avellaneda" [?]). The context within which the reader turns to the poems that precede Chapter I is that of the specification of a series of defects in contemporary literature, the articulation of a set of literary principles governing Cervantes' writing of the book, and the enunciation of a specific literary purpose for having written the book. The frame of reference is so far exclusively and specifically *literary*. It would be difficult to overestimate the significance of this initial orientation. The Prologue partakes of both conclusion and introduction; i.e., it stands in significant relationship to both the beginning and the end of the novel since it constitutes the effort of the author, at the *conclusion* of his text, to position the reader with respect to the *beginning* of the text.

A detailed examination of the parodic prefatory poems would add nothing to our understanding of the thrust and scope of the irony. The poems simply prepare the reader for the appearance of a comic protagonist, and the ridicule is much nearer the surface than in either the Prologue or the text itself.

The First Sally

Chapter I

19.   They will try to tell you that his surname was Quijada or Quesada—there is some difference of opinion among those who have written on the subject—but according to the most likely conjectures we are to understand that it was really Quejana. *But all this means very little so far as our story is concerned, providing that in the telling of it we do not depart one iota from the truth.* (25–26)

The irony produced by the internal contradiction between "the truth" in this biography and the uncertainty as to the biographee's name calls into question the seriousness of "truth."

20. the famous Feliciano de Silva, whose *lucid prose style* and involved conceits were as precious to him as pearls (26)

The internal contradiction is made explicit by the example of unclear prose that follows this remark and is then overtly drawn in "Aristotle himself would not have been able to understand them."

21. the village curate, who was *a learned man*, a graduate of Sigüenza (26)

The irony in this characterization of the curate depends upon the reader's knowledge of the status of the *universidades menores*, objects of satire in the period.

22. he had made up his mind that he was henceforth to be known as Don Quixote, which, as has been stated, has led the authors of this *veracious* history to assume that *his real name must undoubtedly have been Quijada*, and not Quesada as others would have it. (29)

The internal contradiction between "his surname ... was really Quejana" and "his real name must undoubtedly have been Quijada" now clearly ironizes "truth" and "veracious" as used by the narrator.

23. He [praised] the author for [terminating] the book with the promise of [that] interminable adventure. . . . (*26)

The contradiction in "terminating" (*acabar*) the book with an "interminable adventure" (*inacabable*) points up Don Quixote's unawareness of the lack of unity and coherence in novels like *Belianís*, as the suppression of momentary doubts as to its believability points up his insensitivity to the lack of verisimilitude: "He was not at ease in his mind over those wounds that Don Belianís gave and received; for no matter how great the surgeons who treated him, the poor fellow must have been left with his face and his entire body covered with marks and scars. Nevertheless. . . ."

51

Irony helps to underline the opposition established in Chapter I between Cervantes' esthetic principles, as set forth in the Prologue, and Don Quixote's predilections. Don Quixote is presented as confidently unaware that his morion and his horse are inadequate and that his expectations are unrealistic. His image of himself is patently absurd: "That knight who can never be praised enough, Don Quixote." On another level, the author's pretended unawareness of the requirements of "true" history and his inconsistency concerning the name of his protagonist keep the "fictionality" of the narrative in the foreground. In the phrase "a learned man, a graduate of Sigüenza," the *pseudovictim* of the irony is the narrator, "unaware" that "a graduate of Sigüenza" does not denote "a learned man." The *object* of the irony is Sigüenza, and, by extension, all of the *universidades menores*. Sigüenza is devalued through implied overpraise. The identification of the curate as an object of the irony is more problematical. He may or may not be "learned," since the ironic disparity only contrasts, strictly speaking, the *presumption* of equivalence between the two terms with the reader's knowledge that the presumption is mistaken, and does not establish their incompatibility.

Chapter II

24.   "Undoubtedly," he is saying, "in the days to come, when the true history of my famous deeds is published, the learned chronicler who records them, when he comes to describe my first sally so early in the morning, will put down something like this: 'No sooner had the rubicund Apollo spread over the face of the broad and spacious earth the gilded filaments of his beauteous locks, and no sooner had the little singing birds of painted plumage greeted with their sweet and mellifluous harmony the coming of the Dawn, who, leaving the soft couch of her jealous spouse, now showed herself to mortals at all the doors and balconies of the horizon that bounds La Mancha—no sooner had this happened than the famous knight, Don Quixote de la Mancha, forsaking his own downy bed and mounting his famous steed, Rocinante, fared forth and began riding over the ancient and famous Campo de Montiel.'"

And this was the truth, for he was indeed riding over that stretch of plain. (31)

The irony of Don Quixote's version of the narrative lies in the specific implicit contrast with Cervantes' narrative as well as with the contrast between any objective account and his own version. The irony of the narrator's comment lies in the pretended unawareness which it implies of the outrageously inappropriate style adopted by Don Quixote. Don Quixote's self-portrait is amplified here and below: "the famous knight, Don Quixote de la Mancha," "my famous exploits," "exploits worthy of being engraved in bronze," etc.

The rest of the chapter—the arrival at the inn, Don Quixote's reception by the prostitutes and the innkeeper, and the meal—is built upon the irony in a series of double meanings. Three key words are introduced, in successive stages of the action, which function both on the level of the protagonist's chivalric fantasy and on that of the prosaic reality in which the action takes place. The series begins and ends with two nonverbal stimuli which also function on both levels:

25.

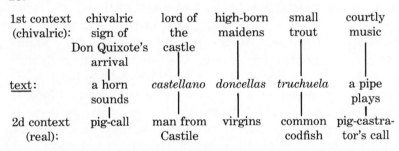

1st context (chivalric):	chivalric sign of Don Quixote's arrival	lord of the castle	high-born maidens	small trout	courtly music
text:	a horn sounds	*castellano*	*doncellas*	*truchuela*	a pipe plays
2d context (real):	pig-call	man from Castile	virgins	common codfish	pig-castrator's call

Cervantes presents Don Quixote's initial contact with others in terms of the inherent ambiguity of language itself. Not only do the characters disagree as to the nature of reality (giants/windmills); they simply do not understand one another. As befits the victim of irony, Don Quixote is "confidently unaware of the very possibility of there being a . . . level or point of view that invalidates his own":[7] "all of which confirmed Don Quixote in the belief that this was indeed a famous castle, for what was this if not music that they were playing for him? The fish was trout, the bread was of the finest, the wenches were ladies, and the innkeeper was the castellan. He was convinced that he had been right in his resolve to sally forth and roam the world at large" (35).

Chapter III

The innkeeper gives Don Quixote an account of his own chivalric activities:

> 26.   *He himself*, the landlord added, when he was a young man, *had followed the same honorable calling.* He had gone through various parts of the world seeking adventures. . . . He had done many wrongs, cheated many widows, ruined many maidens, and swindled not a few minors. . . . (36–37)

A generous or sentimental reader might wish to allege that Don Quixote's failure to perceive the irony in the innkeeper's initial statement is due to an innocent proclivity to expect the best from everyone he meets, to believe that others' motives are as pure and honorable as such a reader perceives Don Quixote's own to be. But the innkeeper goes on to describe quite straightforwardly his lawless, antichivalric activity. The words he uses are explicit and unequivocal. Don Quixote's acceptance of the innkeeper's mock-heroic speech is based entirely upon its *stylistic* conformity to a proper account of chivalric activity, i.e., upon the form divorced from the content. At this point the reader should recall that "above all, [Don Quixote] cherished an admiration for Rinaldo of Montalbán, especially as he beheld him sallying forth from his castle to rob all those that crossed his path" (27). This analysis corroborates my assessment in chapter 2 of the initial presentation of Don Quixote as a would-be author who is attracted by the style of the worst novels of chivalry. He is clearly

7. Douglas C. Muecke, *The Compass of Irony*, p. 20. Subsequent references to this work, upon which this chapter depends heavily, appear in parentheses in the text.

motivated by esthetic, not ethical, considerations, and he is characterized by a lack of esthetic sensibility diametrically opposed to the desirable norm enunciated by Cervantes in the Prologue, exemplified in the narrative style to this point, and ratified explicitly in authorial commentary: "hogs—for, without any apology, that is what they were" (32). I can see no extension or variation of the pattern of irony in the encounter with the muleteers or the knighting of Don Quixote in the rest of the chapter.

Chapter IV

The episode involving Juan Haldudo and Andrés merits our close inspection as (1) the first adventure of Don Quixote involving a person who is really in need, and hence the place to test the conviction fostered by the text that his orientation is essentially esthetic (he wants to be seen as a famous knight-errant) and only incidentally ethical (knights-errant right wrongs); (2) a clear point at which the various mutually exclusive interpretations diverge; and (3) an example of subtle, sustained irony.

27.   The knight had not gone far when from a hedge on his right hand he heard the sound of faint moans as of someone in distress.
       "Thanks be to Heaven," he at once exclaimed, "for the favor it has shown me by providing me so soon with an opportunity to fulfill the obligations that I owe to my profession, a chance to pluck the fruit of my worthy desires." (41–42)

Don Quixote's initial reaction to this encounter with human suffering is to thank God for the opportunity it affords him to demonstrate his own worth. He comes in sight of Andrés, "who [is] uttering the cries, and *not without reason.* . . ." The ironic understatement (litotes) can only minimize the effect of the whipping on the reader, reducing the possible pathos of the episode. Don Quixote obliges Juan Haldudo to untie Andrés, and Haldudo offers to take the boy home and pay him. The logic of the exchange that follows is worth noting:

28.

Andrés:	I go home with him!. . . No, sir, . . . for once he has me alone he'll flay me like a St. Bartholomew.
Don Q.:	He will do nothing of the sort. . . . It is sufficient for me to command, and he out of respect will obey. Since he has sworn to me by the order of knighthood which he has received, I shall let him go free.
	. . .
Andrés:	My master . . . has never received any order of knighthood whatsoever.
Don Q.:	That makes little difference, . . . in view of the fact that every man is the son of his works.
Andrés:	Of what works is he the son, seeing that he refuses me the pay for my sweat and labor? (43)

As often happens in the novel, the dialogue is interrupted at the point of impasse. By Don Quixote's own logic, Juan Haldudo will not behave honorably. The consequences of his disastrous intervention will thus be the result of blindness, not ingenuousness, and the distinction is crucial. The result: "[Juan Haldudo] seized the lad's arm and bound him to the tree again and flogged him within an inch of his life" (44).[8]

Should any doubt remain concerning the perspective from which Cervantes has designed the episode to be viewed, it is

8. More complex retroactive ironies can be extremely subtle in Cervantes. For example, "every man is the son of his works" suggests the possibility of a profound revision of the meaning of "I . . . am but Don Quixote's stepfather" (Prologue), which first seemed to mean only "historian." Later passages of the novel may highlight the folkloric connotations of "stepfather" (harsh, judgmental). At the same time, "every man is the son of his works" may also be seen as an allusion to the peculiar process by which Don Quixote may be said to create Cid Hamete: "The knight invents a chronicler, who is at the same time an enchanter, and he sets diligently about believing in him. In a certain sense, then, Cid Hamete arises from the conviction of Don Quixote that such a chronicler must exist" (Riley, *Cervantes's Theory of the Novel*, p. 329). Thus "every man is the son of his works," and Cid Hamete is the work of Don Quixote. Furthermore, Don Quixote's observation after his defeat by Sansón Carrasco: "Each man is the architect of his own fortune" (943) expresses from the point of view of responsibility (*post*) what "every man is the son of his works" expresses from the point of view of freedom (*ante*).

It will not be my practice here to pursue these revisions beyond the effects which they can be shown to have upon the limits, targets, and stability of the irony, and hence upon Cervantes' strategies. It is important in any event to remember Wayne Booth's observation that "mystery" in the first reading of any novel is replaced by "irony" in the second (*The Rhetoric of Fiction*, pp. 255–56).

dispelled by the transparent irony of the passage that immediately follows:

29. But for all that, he went away weeping, and his master
     stood laughing at him.
        *Such was the manner in which the valorous knight
     righted this particular wrong.* Don Quixote was quite
     content with the way everything had turned out; it
     seemed to him that he had made a very fortunate and
     noble beginning with his deeds of chivalry, and he was
     very well satisfied with himself as he jogged along in the
     direction of his native village, talking to himself in a low
     voice all the while.
        "Well may'st thou call thyself fortunate today, above
     all other women on earth, O fairest of the fair, Dulcinea
     del Toboso! Seeing that it has fallen to thy lot to hold
     subject and submissive to thine every wish and pleasure
     so valiant and renowned a knight as Don Quixote de la
     Mancha is and shall be, who, as everyone knows, . . . has
     righted the greatest wrong and grievance that injustice
     ever conceived or cruelty ever perpetrated, by snatching
     the lash from the hand of the merciless foeman who was
     so unreasonably flogging that *tender [infant]*." (44)

Even if one disregards the thrust of the foregoing context, it is
clear that the initial affirmation in this passage simply cannot be
taken as an expression of Cosmic or General irony underlining
the paradox of the evil results which sometimes issue from good
intentions. The adjective *valorous* counts too heavily against
Don Quixote, for it is not an attribution that has been suggested
by his activity in the episode; rather, it is a mocking echo of his
vain self-description a moment before: "I am the valorous Don
Quixote de la Mancha, righter of wrongs and injustices" (43).
Confident unawareness and vanity are inseparably linked in the
phrases "quite content with the way everything had turned out"
and "very well satisfied with himself" and in the passage in
which Don Quixote congratulates Dulcinea on her good fortune.
The final note of irony is Don Quixote's overstatement—*tender
[infant]*—to characterize the fifteen-year-old Andrés.[9]

   9. Cf. Oscar Mandel: "The episode of Juan Haldudo and the boy Andrew
constitutes actually the sharpest piece of irony against Don Quijote of the
whole novel": "The Function of the Norm in *Don Quijote*," p. 162.

Appreciation of the humor of the episode that follows—Don Quixote's defeat at the hands of the merchants—depends upon the reader's adopting the proper perspective toward the episode of Andrés. The pity that the bare narration of the drubbing Don Quixote receives would naturally elicit is thus forestalled.

Chapter V

30. "Señor Quijana," he said (*for such must have been Don Quixote's real name* when he was in his right senses and before he had given up the life of a quiet country gentleman to become a knight-errant). . . . (48)

This third resolution of Don Quixote's name (cf. "it was really Quejana" [26]; "his real name must undoubtedly have been Quijada" [29]) reduces the historical rigor of the "true history" to a shambles.

Chapter VI

The first sally is framed by two discussions of contemporary literature: the Prologue and Chapter VI. Despite the touch of irony with which the curate is introduced in Chapter I ("a learned man, a graduate of Sigüenza"), it is undeniable that he takes on total literary authority in Chapter VI. His easy laughter at the housekeeper's superstition is shared by the reader, and the irony that it is the housekeeper and the niece who represent obscurantist "inquisitional" religion in the auto-da-fé, while the curate's judgments are wholly esthetic, works in his favor. His esthetic principles coincide exactly with those Cervantes has already revealed as his own: condemnation of "diabolic and involved conceits" and "stiffness and dryness of . . . style," praise of dialogue which is "clear and polished, the character and condition of the one who is speaking being observed with much propriety and understanding," and a commitment to verisimilitude.[10] The identification eventually becomes explicit: "Ah, that fellow Cervantes and I have been friends these many years" (57).

10. I hope the reader will forgive the omission of a discussion of the irony in the curate's praise (ironic blame) of *Tirante el blanco*. Interpretation of the passage involves many difficulties and would in no way advance our purposes here.

31.   "Here, Señor Licentiate," she said, "take this and sprinkle well, that no enchanter of the many these books contain may remain here to cast a spell on us for wishing to banish them from the world." (52)

The housekeeper is unaware that enchanters do not exist. The fact that she suffers from the same delusion as Don Quixote, whom she wishes to cure, constitutes a further irony.

32.   "By the holy orders that I have received," the curate declared, "since Apollo was Apollo, since the Muses were Muses and poets were poets, *so droll* and absurd *a book as this has not been written*; in its own way it is unique among all those of its kind that have seen the light of day, and he who has not read it does not know what he has missed. Give it to me, my friend, for I am more pleased at having found it than if they had presented me with a cassock of Florentine cloth." (56)

Devaluation through hyperbolic praise can be risky, and here it needs the internal contradiction of "so droll and absurd" to ensure that it is perceived as irony. Even so, Cervantes is careful to have the curate apply it only to a notoriously bad book.

Conclusions

> Let him bear it and hold his peace who is rash
> enough to attempt more than his strength
> will warrant.
> (Part I, Chapter XLIV, 401)

Cervantes' literary principles are clearly established: "imitation," verisimilitude, clear and unpretentious style, attention to decorum. Most novels of chivalry and much other contemporary literature are alleged to lack these qualities. Don Quixote's madness results from an uncritical submission to the worst of these books—an overdose of them—and he is the consistent victim of Cervantes' irony, fulfilling all of the three formal requirements for the role of ironic victim as they have been defined by D. C. Muecke: (1) "Irony is a double-layered . . . phenomenon. At the

lower level is the situation ... as it appears to the victim. ... At the
upper level is the situation as it appears to the observer"; (2)
"There is always some kind of opposition between the two levels.
... What the victim thinks may be contradicted by what the
observer knows" (pp. 19–20). In the episode with Andrés, for
example, this is what Don Quixote thinks: "today [I have] righted
the greatest wrong and grievance that injustice ever conceived
..." (44), and this is what the observer knows: "he flogged him
within an inch of his life." (3) "There is in irony an element of
'innocence'; a victim is confidently unaware of the very possibility of there being an upper level" (Muecke, p. 20). After Don
Quixote leaves the scene, the narrator stresses the knight's
confident unawareness: Don Quixote was "quite content with
the way everything had turned out, ... very well satisfied with
himself ..." (44).

If the *victim* of irony is the "the person whose 'confident unawareness' has directly involved him in an ironic situation," the
object or *target* of irony is "what one is ironical about. ... The
object of irony may be a person (including the ironist himself), an
attitude, a belief, a social custom or institution, a philosophical
system, a religion, even a whole civilization, even life itself"
(Muecke, p. 34).

The *victims* of irony in the Prologue and the first sally are:

1. the narrator (pseudovictim): 2, 5, 6, 7, 8, 9, 10, 11, 12, 14,
   15, 19, 20, 21, 22, 24, 30;
2. the "friend" (pseudovictim): 16;
3. Don Quixote: 20, 23, 24, 25, 26, 28, 29;
4. the housekeeper: 31;
5. the curate (pseudovictim): 32.

The *objects* (targets) of irony are:

1. the following esthetic flaws: mediocre and pretentious
   prefatory verse 6, 12, 16; violations of decorum 10, 24; false
   erudition 8, 9, 11, 16; confusion of verisimilitude with
   pseudohistoricity 19, 22, 30; pretentiousness or obscurity of
   style 20, 24; lack of unity and/or coherence 23, 32;
2. those who are insensitive to any of these: 20, 23;

3. the vices implicitly associated with the esthetic flaws: hypocrisy 10, 16; vanity 16, 24; sloth 16; ambition 16;

4. any authors to whom the vices in 3 and/or the consequent esthetic failures in 1 may be ascribed: 12, 24;

5. the *universidades menores*: 21;

6. Don Quixote as he exemplifies 2: 20, 23, 26; as he exemplifies any of the vices of 3 in his "esthetic" endeavor: e.g., vanity 24, 29; and as one of those included in 4: 24;

7. superstition: 31.

The *ironists* are:

1. the narrator: 2, 5, 6, 7, 8, 9, 10, 11, 12, 14, 15, 19, 20, 21, 22, 23, 24, 29, 30;
2. the "friend": 16;
3. the innkeeper: 26;
4. the curate: 32.

Two further observations are pertinent. The first is a general observation by Muecke: "One of the odd things about irony is that it regards assumptions as presumptions and therefore innocence as guilt. Simple ignorance is safe from irony, but *ignorance compounded with the least degree of confidence counts as intellectual hubris* and is a punishable offence" (p. 30, emphasis mine). The second is Booth's perception that in works where the irony is based upon a consistent set of norms (stable irony), neither the implied author nor the reader is intended to be the victim. They are expected to share the same perspective on the text.[11]

According to Muecke's scheme, "in Overt Irony the victim or the reader or both are meant to see the ironist's real meaning at once" (p. 54). Specific Irony involves "single victims or victimizations, single exposures of aberrancy in a world otherwise safely moving on the right track . . ." (p. 119).

The strategy of the Prologue to Part I and the first sally is Overt, Specific (i.e., limited), Comic irony in the service of satire, and it exhibits the following principal tactics from among those listed by Muecke (pp. 64–98):

11. Wayne C. Booth, *A Rhetoric of Irony*, p. 233.

1. blaming in order to praise: 14;
2. praising in order to blame: 8, 9, 10, 20, 21, 32;
3. internal contradiction: 5, 10, 16, 19, 20, 22, 23, 26, 28, 29, 30, 32:
4. stylistic signals, such as (a) the "ironical manner": 15 and (b) stylistic "placing": 24, 25;
5. the ironist's self-disparagement: 2, 7, 14;
6. overstatement: 15, 29;
7. understatement: ("not without reason" p. 16);
8. ambiguity: 25.

Since the literary irony is consistent, overt, coherent, and "justifiable" (cf. the *Aprobaciones* to Part II), the only possible avenue for extension of the irony and/or satire beyond the esthetic and moral flaws I have identified is allegory. The contention that Cervantes is aiming at another target (the state, the religious establishment, contemporary ideology, the human condition) would have to be supported by a consistent set of covert connections together with the specification of the rhetorical signals necessary for their recognition. Anything short of that must be considered incidental (e.g., the irony directed at the *universidades menores*) and not essential to the central thrust. It would also appear that only with considerable difficulty, and through powerful rhetorical signals, could the author undermine the authority of a character like the curate, who has become his ally in the principal satiric endeavor. On the other hand, any fallibility in his judgment which is *not* meant to undermine his basic authority will need to be circumscribed in order not to jeopardize that authority.[12]

I should add that I see no evidence in the first six chapters to support the common notion that Don Quixote functions, even briefly, as an ingénu or innocent, exposing the "woven complexities of hypocrisy and rationalization" or piercing "the protective tissues of convention and idées reçues" in others (Muecke, p. 91). Rather, he is consistently presented as the victim of the irony of the narrator, the other characters, and the situations that his behavior produces.

12. See Sheldon Sacks, *Fiction and the Shape of Belief*, pp. 119–33.

We have seen how Don Quixote, as an object of irony, is linked to the works of literature that are also the objects of Cervantes' ironic satire. Don Quixote imitates the heroes of the novels of chivalry, but Cervantes aligns him with their authors and devotees. Like them, he is vain, pompous, and gullible, and lacks esthetic sensibility.

II. THE SECOND SALLY

Specific Comic Irony

Are there differences in the victims, targets, or scope of the irony in the rest of Part I? The identification of Don Quixote with readers and authors of novels of chivalry is now firmly established, and he is the principal target or object of the narrator's irony throughout the second sally. The introduction of another gullible reader, Juan Palomeque (Chapter XXXII), allows Cervantes to reintroduce the issue briefly on its original terms, but the primary development of this theme is in the extended exchange between the canon and the curate, which is not presented ironically. The exchange parallels the serious advice given by Cervantes' "friend" in the Prologue. It should be noted that the second sally is framed by the literary "inquisition" of Chapter VI and these discussions in Chapters XLVII–L, exactly as the first was bounded by the Prologue and Chapter VI, thus underlining the persistence of the literary frame of reference.

An important difference between the two sallies lies in the relative predominance in the first of the mode of irony which Muecke calls "Impersonal," in which the narrator is the ironist, and in the second of "Dramatized" irony, where there is no ironist (pp. 64–98). The progression is a logical one, for once the author has clearly established the norms of his created world and characterized the typical deviations from them, he can withdraw somewhat with the expectation that the reader will perceive unaided the self-betrayal of the characters in action.

Before attempting to establish the parameters of the irony of which Don Quixote, and now Sancho, are the objects in the second sally, some additions to the list of ironists, as well as to the

lists of victims and objects (targets), should be noted. Several of
the characters participate in the irony of pretended agreement
with or encouragement of Don Quixote: Vivaldo (93–96), the curate (252), Dorotea (258–59). More interesting are the instances in
which Sancho and Don Quixote are ironical. Sancho functions
both as conscious ironist vis-à-vis Don Quixote and as ingénu. In
pretending that his story of Lope Ruiz and La Torralba has an
ending, one which has been spoiled by Don Quixote's failure to
keep count of the goats as they cross the river, Sancho is of course
being ironical at his master's expense:

33.　　"There, what did I tell you? You should have kept
　　　　better count. Well, then, by God, the story's ended, for
　　　　there is no going on with it."
　　　　　"How can that be?" said the knight. "Is it so essential to
　　　　know the exact number of goats that if I lose count of one
　　　　of them you cannot tell the rest of the tale?"
　　　　　"No, sir, I cannot by any means," said Sancho; "for
　　　　when I asked your Grace to tell me how many goats had
　　　　been rowed across and you replied that you did not know,
　　　　at that very instant everything that I was about to say
　　　　slipped my memory; and you may take my word for it, it
　　　　was very good and you would have liked it."
　　　　　"So," said Don Quixote, "the story is ended, is it?"
　　　　　"As much ended as my own mother is," Sancho replied.
　　　　(151)

The following exchange from the same chapter also seems to me
to be conscious irony on Sancho's part, though it is possible that
his "praise" of Don Quixote is ingenuous:

34.　　"for I may tell you, Sancho, that there is no calling any-
　　　　where more dangerous than that of adventurer."
　　　　　"That is the truth," said Sancho, "seeing that *[only the]*
　　　　sound of fulling hammers can disturb and agitate the
　　　　heart of so valiant a knightly adventurer as is your
　　　　Grace." (*156)

Cervantes also contrives to have Sancho produce statements
typical of the ingénu, but which function at the same time as
dramatized ironic self-betrayal:

35. "Señor Don Quixote," he exclaimed, "I swear and vow
     that you are not in your right senses!" (261)

According to Sancho, Don Quixote is crazy for not accepting
Micomicona's offer of marriage. Like the ingénu, he reveals the
truth without knowing it himself, but at the same time he betrays the blindness which the prospect of getting his island always produces in him. As the narrator will later remark, after
the episode of the wineskins, "Sancho awake was worse than his
master asleep, such had been the effect of the promises Don
Quixote had made him" (316). A purer example of Sancho as
ingénu is his rustic praise of Aldonza Lorenzo in Chapter XXV
(204–5)—a perfect example of Muecke's "praise for having undesirable qualities" (p. 67).

The emergence of Don Quixote as ironist is a matter of capital
importance in Cervantes' strategies of irony. Ingenuousness or
gullibility and the ironic perspective are mutually exclusive, and
if the latter is not to drive out the former, each must be circumscribed within a different sphere of operation, or else it must
be clear what conditions are responsible for the loss of perspective. We have seen that it is Sancho's interest in the island that
fosters his gullibility. Don Quixote's capacity for self-deception is
much greater, and as a result he is demonstrably ironic only once
that I have observed in the *Quixote* of 1605—in the conscious
rhetorical irony of the speech on Arms and Letters:

36. "At times [the soldier's] nakedness is such that a *slashed*
     doublet serves him at once as shirt and uniform; and in
     midwinter, in the open country, it is his habit to protect
     himself against the inclemencies of the heavens with
     nothing more than the breath from his mouth, which,
     *inasmuch as it emerges from an empty place, must obvi-
     ously, contrary to all the laws of nature, come out cold.*
     True, he looks forward to the coming of night that he may
     find a respite from all these discomforts in *the bed that
     awaits him, which, unless it is through some fault of his
     own, will never offend by being too narrow; for he may
     measure out upon the earth as many feet as he likes for his
     couch and then may toss and turn in it to his heart's
     content, without fear of the sheets slipping off.*

> *"Comes then the day and hour when he is to take his professional degree;* comes then the day of battle; and *then it is they place upon his head a doctor's cap* made of lint, by way of healing the wound inflicted by some bullet. . . ."* (340–41)

Even this restricted use of overt oratorical irony by Don Quixote moves him away from ridicule towards pity; the speech on Arms and Letters is, in fact, the first occasion in the novel when we are told that he is an object of pity (343).

Outside the larger strategies of irony, examples of incidental irony are relatively few.

37. a good man—*if this title may be applied to one who is poor—* (60)

In this example, the pretended doubt of the narrator ironizes the confusion of the moral and the monetary.

Maritornes is the object of a particular kind of incidental irony of which Fielding, who acknowledged that he wrote "in imitation of the manner of Cervantes," was fond:

38. Serving in the inn, also, was a lass from Asturia, broad-faced, flat-headed, and with a snub nose; she was blind in one eye and could not see very well out of the other. *To be sure, her bodily graces made up for her other defects*: she measured not more than seven palms from head to foot, and, being slightly hunchbacked, she had to keep looking at the ground a good deal more than she liked. *This gentle creature.* . . . (115)

This tactic of explicit internal contradiction appears again in the ironic treatment of Maritornes' sexual behavior. Of her promise to sleep with the muleteer, he tells us that

39. she never made such a promise without keeping it, *even though it was in a forest and without witnesses, for she prided herself greatly upon being a lady and did not look upon it as any disgrace to be a servant in an inn,* for, as she

was in the habit of saying, it was misfortunes and ill luck that had brought her to such a state. (117)

The irony of the narrator's pretended unawareness of the incompatibility of "whore" and "lady" (*hidalga*), and of the direction in which "in a forest and without witnesses" moves, includes the broader conventional target of the Asturian presumption of *hidalguía*.

Finally, the innkeeper's wife is the victim of dramatized incidental irony. The ambiguity of the veiled *double entendre* in the talk about the wife's "tail" which the barber borrows for his disguise has no object beyond the off-color insinuations:

40. "By the sign of the holy cross!" she cried, *"you are not going to make use of my tail* as a beard any longer. Give it back to me at once. *It is a shame the way that thing of my husband's is all the time on the floor*—I mean the comb that I used to stick into that pretty tail of mine." (274)

   "this other gentleman comes along and carries off my tail and gives it back to me with more than two cuartillos' worth of damage done to it, all stripped of its hair and of no further use for my husband's purpose." (317)

To return to the consideration of the larger ironic strategies of Part I, there are, in the episodes of the second sally, a number of clear examples which indicate that the narrator's ironic perspective on Don Quixote has not changed:

41. the whole story of the *life and [miracles]* of our famous Spaniard, Don Quixote, light and mirror of the chivalry of La Mancha, the first in our age and in these calamitous times to devote himself to the hardships and exercises of knight-errantry and to go about righting wrongs, succoring widows, and protecting damsels—damsels such as those who, mounted upon their palfreys and with riding-whip in hand, in full possession of their virginity, were in the habit of going from mountain to mountain and from valley to valley; for unless there were some villain, some rustic with an ax and hood, or some monstrous giant to force them, there were in times past *maiden ladies who* at the end of eighty years, during all

which time they had not slept for a single day beneath a roof, *would go to their graves as virginal as [the mothers who bore them]*. (*71)

This is a rather complex ironic sequence, involving a combination of (1) praising in order to blame or ridicule ("life and miracles") and (2) pretended error, resulting in (3) internal contradiction ("as virginal as the mothers who bore them"). The juxtaposition of the characterization of Don Quixote as "the first in our age ... to devote himself to ... protecting damsels" and "damsels such as those who ... would go to their graves as virginal as the mothers who bore them" causes the focus to shift from the potential ethical field of observation ("righting wrongs") to the esthetic field of the inverisimilitude of bad novels of chivalry. It is thus that the phrase which follows the passage acquires ironic force: "If I speak of these things, it is for the reason that *in this* and in all other respects *our gallant Don Quixote is deserving of constant memory and praise . . .*" (71).

The narrator can also, of course, refer ironically to previous episodes, secure in the knowledge that the reader has been properly oriented by their presentation:

42.   Sancho had told the curate and the barber about the adventure of the galley slaves, [*which his master had concluded with so much glory*]. . . . (*255–56)

More interesting, however, are the examples of dramatized irony in these chapters, which confirm that the author's perspective on Don Quixote coincides with that of his narrators. The dramatized irony of examples 24, 26, 27, and 29 from the first sally establishes the same point, but the first two and the last of these are complicated by the presence of an ironist in the text—the narrator, the innkeeper, and again the narrator, respectively. The following cases of the dramatized irony of self-betrayal are, like 27, products of the unmediated efforts of Cervantes.

In the first example Don Quixote again betrays the scant attention that he pays to what others say, as in 26 and 28, preferring to continue blindly his own train of thought:

43.   "But I must warn you that even though you see me in the
      greatest peril in the world, you are not to lay hand upon
      your sword to defend me, unless it be that those who
      attack me are rabble and men of low degree. . . ."
         "Most certainly, sir," replied Sancho, "your Grace shall
      be very well obeyed in this; all the more so for the reason
      that I myself am of a peaceful disposition and not fond of
      meddling in the quarrels and feuds of others. However,
      when it comes to protecting my own person, I shall not
      take account of those laws of which you speak, seeing
      that all laws, human and divine, permit each one to
      defend himself whenever he is attacked."
         "I am willing to grant you that," assented Don Quixote,
      "but in this matter of defending me against gentlemen
      you must restrain your natural impulses." (65–66)

   The example that follows is a particularly damning betrayal of
the discrepancy between the noble sentiments expressed by Don
Quixote and his practice in the concrete situation:

44.   "In order, Sancho, that you may see the good that
      there is in knight-errantry and how speedily those who
      follow the profession, no matter what the nature of their
      service may be, come to be honored and esteemed in the
      eyes of the world, I would have you here in the company
      of these good folk seat yourself at my side, that you may
      be even as I who am your master and natural lord, and
      eat from my plate and drink from where I drink; for of
      knight-errantry one may say the same as of love: that it
      makes all things equal." (80)

When Sancho declines the offer, Don Quixote reveals the hypocrisy of his offer of equality: "'But for all that,' said Don Quixote,
'you must sit down; for whosoever humbleth himself, him God
will exalt.' And, laying hold of his squire's arm, he compelled him
to take a seat beside him." The irony of the reference to humility
is particularly pointed when set against "honored and esteemed
in the eyes of the world." Compare also the point of Sancho's
story in Chapter XXXI of Part II, the punch line of which is: "Sit
down, you stupid ass, for wherever I sit will be the head of the
table to you" (714).

69

Cervantes has a very fine sense of the light touch necessary to tip the balance between what is acceptable in a given situation and what constitutes the victim's self-betrayal. Don Quixote's response to Dorotea's hyperbolic praise of his prowess is a good example:

45.   "That will be enough!" said Don Quixote. "Let me hear no more words of praise! For I am opposed to any kind of adulation. . . ."

So far, so good, but the victim of the irony of self-betrayal always compulsively goes too far: " . . . and even though this be no fawning, *such talk* for all of that *offends my chaste ears*" (255).

As a final example of Don Quixote's self-betrayal, let us look at the way in which Cervantes handles the reappearance of Andrés, keeping in mind the treatment of the initial encounter as analyzed earlier (pp. 55–58):

46.   As they were engaged in their repast, a lad came along the highway and, after studying them all attentively, ran over to Don Quixote and clasped him around the legs, weeping copiously.
      "Ah sir! Do you not know me, your Grace? Look at me well, for I am the lad Andrés that your Grace freed from the oak tree to which he was bound."
      The knight then recognized him and, taking him by the hand, he turned to the others and said, "In order that your Worships may see how important it is to have knights-errant in the world to right the wrongs and injuries done by the insolent and evil beings who inhabit it, you may know that some while ago, as I was passing through a wood, I heard certain pitiful cries and moans as from one who was afflicted and in distress. I then, as was my duty, went to the place. . . .
      "The short of it was, I compelled the peasant to release the boy and made him promise to take him home and pay him every real of what he owed him, and perfumed into the bargain. Is not that all true, Andrés, my son? *Did you not note how imperiously I commanded him to do that and with what humility he promised to carry out all my orders and instructions?* Speak up and tell these ladies and gentlemen, clearly and in a straightforward manner, just what happened; for I would have them see and be con-

vinced that I was right when I said that it is very useful
to have knights-errant going up and down the high-
roads." (271–72)

Don Quixote's speech, particularly in the initial and final
clauses, constitutes a classic demonstration of "confident unawareness." The humiliation which he suffers as a result is
exactly proportionate to the disparity between his claim concerning the need for knights-errant in the world and the opinion
of Andrés: "your Grace is to blame, . . . no misfortune could be so
great as that which comes of being helped by you. May God curse
you and all the knights-errant that were ever born into this
world!" (272–73). Clemencín was of course correct in noting that
"this recrimination contradicts the embrace and tears of Andrés
which were described previously, and which seemed rather signs
of gratitude than of complaint. And his words as he leaves . . . are
even more contradictory."[13] The fact is that character motivation has here been subordinated to authorial strategy. The
justification for Andrés' initial behavior lies in the self-betrayal
that I have italicized in Don Quixote's speech and in the negative
qualities, already abundantly manifested, that it reveals.

Sancho, too, is a victim of the irony of self-betrayal. We have
already seen one example of this (35), and I discussed in chapter 2
the irony of his perception of Teresa's inadequacy to be queen
while remaining blind to his own inadequacy to be king. Sancho's
"confident unawareness" at times equals that of his master, as
the narrator indicates in his comments on the squire's self-
betrayal in the following passage:

47.   He also told how Don Quixote, in case he had a favorable
       reply from the lady Dulcinea del Toboso, was going to set
       out to make himself an emperor or at least a monarch, for
       so they had agreed between them, this being a very easy
       thing to accomplish in view of his personal worth and the
       might of his arm; and when he had achieved it, he was to
       marry off his squire, who would, of course, be a widower
       by that time, giving him as a wife one of the empress's
       damsels, the heiress to a large and rich estate on *terra*

13. Diego Clemencín, ed., *El ingenioso hidalgo Don Quijote de la Mancha*, p.
1318*n*40.

firma, for he wanted nothing more to do with islands of any kind.

He said all this with so much composure and so little show of judgment, wiping his nose from time to time, that his friends could not but marvel. . . . (215)

Finally, it should be noted that at the close of Part I the narrator once again directs his irony at the inverisimilitude of the novels of chivalry:

48.   the author . . . only asks of his readers that they give it the same credence that the discerning do to those books of chivalry that are so popular in the world today. (460)

The passage follows directly upon the discussion of the blatantly anachronistic documents relating to Don Quixote discovered in the lead box, "which . . . had been found in the crumbling foundation of a very old hermitage that was being rebuilt."[14]

Discussion of the irony in the episodes of the second sally would be incomplete without an examination of a radically different type which involves neither the presence of an ironist in the text nor the characters' self-betrayal: Irony of Events. We thus move from Specific to General Comic irony, from the perspectives of the characters, including the narrator, to that of the author himself, and from the foibles and vices of individuals to the way in which the world inhabited by these individuals works.

General Comic Irony

For an understanding of the strategy involved in the Irony of Events in the world of *Don Quixote*, Norman Knox's revision of Muecke's exposition of the "compass of irony" is essential.[15] Muecke asserted that General Irony "is not primarily corrective

14. Americo Castro's association of these documents with those found at the end of the sixteenth century in the caves of the Sacro Monte in Granada would, if correct, add a touch of satire to the irony, but it would not make of the Benedictine friars the "giants" he takes them for (ibid., pp. 10–102).

15. Knox, "On the Classification of Ironies." Subsequent references to this essay appear in parentheses in the text.

or normative," but paradoxical, as opposed to Specific Irony, which exposes deviations from the ironist's norms. But Knox rejects the distinction, pointing out that General Irony may also be normative and offering as an example Muecke's own quote from Hegel: "God lets men do as they please with their particular passions and interests; but the result is the accomplishment of—not their plans but his, and these differ decidedly from the ends sought by those whom he employs" (Muecke, p. 134). What Knox and Hegel are talking about is, of course, Providence, and the irony involved in the workings of Providence in *Don Quixote* is General Comic irony "in which the appearance of disaster resolves itself into the reality of good fortune" (Knox, p. 53)— when good fortune is deserved. Such irony is also involved when characters are punished by "fortuitous" events or coincidence for their misdeeds or "confident unawareness," thus maintaining the broad balance of justice embraced by the term *comedia* as it was used in the theater of Cervantes' Spain.

There are three major instances of such Irony of Events in *Don Quixote*, Part I. In the first example, Dorotea, reunited with Fernando after the resolution of the problems of the two pairs of lovers, addresses Don Quixote:

49. "Whoever it was that told you, valiant Knight of the Mournful Countenance, that my being had been changed and transformed, was not speaking the truth. It is true that certain fortunate circumstances that have given me more than I could have wished for have worked a change of a sort in me; but *I have not for that reason ceased to be the person that I was before*, and *I still have the same intention that I always did of availing myself of the might of your valiant and invulnerable arm*. And so, my dear sir, I beg you to be so good as to honor once more the father who begot me, and I trust that you will look upon him as a wise and foreseeing man, since with his science he found so ready and reliable a means of aiding me in my trouble. For *I am convinced that if it had not been for you, sir, I should never have had the good fortune that is now mine, and in this I speak the veriest truth*, as most of these worthy folk who are present can testify." (334)

73

Dorotea's tactics in this passage are those of ironic ambiguity. The underlined portions are examples of deceiving with the truth, wherein Dorotea states the facts but pretends that they are true in a sense in which they are not. She is the same as before (but as Dorotea, *not* as Micomicona); she has the same intentions as before (*not* to depend upon Don Quixote's chivalric assistance); and her good fortune has resulted from her relationship with Don Quixote (but *not* from his chivalric activity). Beyond this, however, is the Irony of Events (50) upon which her final verbal irony is based. The irony is that Don Quixote should unwittingly be the agent of the salvation of the very person whom he strives in his madness to save. His instrumentality has nothing to do with his chivalric activity, however. He is the tool of Providence, the workings of which the other characters recognize explicitly: Lucinda tells Fernando that "Heaven, by unaccustomed paths that are dark to us, has placed before me my true husband" (325); the friends of Don Fernando, the curate, and the barber beseech the young nobleman to "reflect that it was not by mere chance, as it might seem, but rather by a special providence of Heaven, that they had all been brought together in a place where they would never have thought they would meet" (328–29). The victim of Dorotea's irony is Don Quixote; the Irony of Events, by contrast, does not have a victim, but rather a beneficiary. It is Dorotea herself for whom "the appearance of disaster resolves into the reality of good fortune."

In the second example of Irony of Events, Don Quixote addresses the innkeeper's daughter in response to Maritornes' request that he give her his hand at the window of the inn:

51. "Lady," he was saying, "take this hand, or better, this avenger of the world's evildoers. The hand of no other woman has ever touched it, not even that of her who holds entire possession of my body. I extend it to thee, not that thou shouldst kiss it, but that thou mayest study the contexture of the sinews, the network of the muscles, the breadth and spaciousness of the veins, from which thou canst deduce how great must be the might of the arm that supports such a hand." (393)

74

The irony is that Don Quixote should be strung up by the very hand that he has just made the sign of his supposed invincibility. Maritornes and the innkeeper's daughter, authors of the deed, are not the engineers of the Irony of Events, but its tools. Don Quixote, in this case the victim of the Irony of Events, has received a precisely applied dose of poetic justice.

The third instance is not related to any specific statement. It is, however, related to the actions of Maritornes and the innkeeper's daughter in the episode just discussed. In the chapter that follows (XLIV), two guests try to leave the inn without paying. The innkeeper remonstrates with them and a fight ensues in which the innkeeper is getting the worst of it. The presentation of the episode maximizes the Irony of Events in which it functions. The focus is not upon the innkeeper, who suffers physically, nor upon his wife, who would logically be the most upset under the circumstances, but upon Maritornes and the daughter, who are the victims of the Irony of Events:

52. His wife and daughter looked about for someone to aid him, but the only person whose attention was not taken up was Don Quixote; so the *innkeeper's daughter* addressed herself to him.

"Sir Knight," she said, "by the power that God has reposed in you, I beg you to succor my poor father. There are two wicked men out there who are beating him to a pulp."

"Lovely damsel," was the knight's measured and phlegmatic response, "your request is at this moment out of place, for I am prevented from entering upon any other adventure until I shall have fulfilled my word and brought to a conclusion the one upon which I am at present embarked. What I may do, however, in order to serve you is this: run and tell your father to sustain this combat as best he may and in no wise to allow himself to be vanquished while I go beg permission. . . ."

"Sinner that I am!" *exclaimed Maritornes* when she heard this, "before your Grace obtains the permission you speak of, my master will be in the other world. . . ."

The princess gave her consent readily enough, and he

75

then, bracing his buckler and grasping his sword, ran out
to the gate of the inn, where the two guests were still
mistreating the landlord. But as he came up, he stopped
short as if perplexed, although *Maritornes* and the landlady kept urging him to help their master and husband,
asking him why he hesitated.

"If I hesitate," said Don Quixote, "it is for the reason
that it is not permitted me to lay hand to sword against
those of the rank of squire; but go call my own squire,
Sancho, for me, for it appertains to him to undertake this
defense and vengeance."

All this took place at the gateway of the inn, where
many most effective blows and punches were being ex-
changed to the great detriment of the landlord as *the
wrath of Maritornes and of the landlady and her daughter
increased.* . . . (400–401)

The irony, of course, is that Maritornes and the innkeeper's
daughter should be frustrated by the very same chivalric madness of Don Quixote that shortly before was the vehicle of their
gratuitous cruelty.

The nature of the irony in these three examples differs from
that in all the episodes previously discussed (e.g., the episode of
Andrés and Juan Haldudo) in that Irony of Events is unforesee-
able and "fortuitous." By contrast, Don Quixote's intervention in
the case of Andrés *produced* the disastrous results. The first two
examples illustrate how the General Comic irony of the workings
of Providence harmonizes with the Specific Comic irony of the
narrator and of authoritative characters. We may note, also, that
the third incident is purely and simply providential and is not
associated with any ironic statement.[16]

16. The allegation of Torrente Ballester (*El "Quijote" como juego*, pp. 142–45)
that this episode is evidence of Don Quixote's consciousness of what is really
happening around him, and of his role-playing, arises, as did Clemencin's perplex-
ity in regard to the reappearance of Andrés (above, p. 71), from a confusion of
authorial strategies with the motivations of the characters. However odd it may
seem (and it is, in fact, obviously ironic) that Don Quixote does settle the fight
through "persuasive reasoning," that is a subordinate moment in the episode and
is really an epilogue, appropriately delayed until the Irony of Events has had its
full effect upon the reader.

Conclusions

> That which is commonly called Fortune ... is nothing
> else but a firm disposition of the Heavens.
>
> (The narrator, *Persiles*, II)

The *victims* of irony in the second sally are:

1. the narrator (pseudovictim): 37, 38, 39, 41, 42, 48;
2. Don Quixote: 33, 43, 44, 45, 46, 49, 51; (pseudovictim): 36;
3. Sancho: 35, 47; (pseudovictim): 33, 34(?);
4. the innkeeper's wife: 40;
5. Maritornes and the innkeeper's daughter: 52;
6. Dorotea (pseudovictim): 49.

The *objects* (targets) of irony are:

1. inverisimilitude: 41, 48;
2. greed/ambition: 35, 47;
3. hypocrisy: 39, 44, 45;
4. vanity: 42, 43, 44, 45, 46, 51;
5. confusion of the moral and the monetary: 37;
6. those who manifest 2, 3, and 4: Sancho 35, 47; Don Quixote 42, 43, 44, 45, 46, 51; Maritornes 39;
7. Maritornes' deformity: 38;
8. gratuitous cruelty of Maritornes and the innkeeper's daughter: 52.

The *ironists* are:

1. the narrator: 37, 38, 39, 41, 42, 48;
2. Vivaldo, the curate, and Dorotea (see pp. 63–64);
3. Sancho: 33, 34(?);
4. Don Quixote: 36;
5. Dorotea: 49.

The strategy of Overt, Specific Comic irony directed at the same or similar targets and employing the same tactics continues throughout the second sally. But there are two important differences in the irony in the second sally: (1) the extent to which Don Quixote and Sancho become the objects of irony not through direct reference to the novels of chivalry—which are criticized without irony by the curate and the canon (Chapters XLVII–L) for precisely the same defects satirized in the Prologue and the first sally—and not through the constant intrusion of the narrator as ironist, but through self-betrayal, and (2) the shift from the predominantly esthetic targets of the first sally to the predominantly ethical ones of the second as the irony moves from the field of observation of literature to that of life.

The operation of the Irony of Events reveals that the world of *Don Quixote* is governed by a benevolent Providence which rewards virtue and punishes vice. Don Quixote is never punished for his virtues, but he consistently suffers the adverse consequences of his vices as the victim of either the irony of others or the Irony of Events. Though Muecke seems to consider him a paradigm of the ingénu (p. 91), I find myself unable to point to a single instance in Part I in which Don Quixote functions in this role.

Nothing in the strategies of the irony of Part I invalidates or calls into question the context provided for the reader by the Prologue (see p. 50). The "soft" critics, who idealize Don Quixote, must show us specifically *where he suffers for his beliefs* and not as a corrective to his vanity, and *where the world is inadequate to his noble desires* and not simply deserving of a modicum of attention from those who aspire to execute great deeds in it. They must show us who the other victims and targets of the irony are and specify the signals by which they can be recognized as such. Meanwhile I must conclude, provisionally at least, that the irony of Part I is a combination of limited and stable Specific Comic irony and the General Comic irony of a beneficent Providence through which, as Auerbach said, "well-founded reality holds madness up to ridicule."[17]

III. THE PROLOGUE (1615) AND THE THIRD SALLY

The Prologue and Preparations for the Third Sally

The orientation of the Prologue to Part II is considerably different from that of its counterpart in *Don Quixote*, Part I. The

17. Auerbach, *Mimesis*, p. 347.

frame of reference is again exclusively literary, but the opposition between Cervantes' novel and those unspecified works of contemporary literature that are the objects of his irony in the first Prologue is replaced by the explicit and specific opposition between Cervantes and Avellaneda. The instances of irony in the second Prologue are rare, but they are clearly directed now at two individuals: Avellaneda and Lope de Vega. The first example is Cervantes' answer to Avellaneda's charge that he had offended Lope in *Don Quixote*, Part I:

53.   It is not likely that I should attack any priest, above all, one that is a familiar of the Holy Office. If he made this statement, as it appears that he did, on behalf of a certain person, then he is utterly mistaken; for the person in question is one whose genius I hold in veneration, [*whose works and whose constant and virtuous activity I admire.*] (*505–6)

This is a fine example of Muecke's "praise for desirable qualities lacking," since it is, as Riquer notes, "an ironic insinuation, given the fact that the life that Lope de Vega led, despite his ordination, was notoriously loose."[18]

Most of Cervantes' response to Avellaneda is straightforward and nonironic, but there is one flash in the following "pretended defense of the victim":

54.   You will likely tell me that I am being too restrained and overmodest, but *it is my belief that affliction is not to be heaped upon the afflicted, and this gentleman must be suffering greatly*, seeing that he does not dare to come out into the open and show himself by the light of day, but must conceal his name and dissemble his place of origin, as if he had been guilty of some treason or act of lese majesty. (506)

The difference between the early chapters of Part I and the corresponding chapters of Part II is even more striking. The

18. Martín de Riquer, ed., *Don Quijote de la Mancha* (Barcelona: Juventud, 1966), p. 536n.

pattern of irony in Part I that involves the pretended agreement of the characters in the novel with Don Quixote, their victim, continues (e.g., Sansón Carrasco: "O mighty Don Quixote de la Mancha, give me your hands; for by the habit of St. Peter that I wear... your Grace is one of the most famous knights-errant that ever have been or ever will be anywhere on this earth" [527]), but Don Quixote now begins to function both as ingénu and as conscious ironist. For example, when the curate, in his ironic pose of pretended agreement, asks him for an opinion concerning the size of the giant Morgante, Don Quixote replies,

55.　　"On this subject of giants . . . opinions differ as to whether or not there ever were any in this world: but the Holy Scriptures, which do not depart from the truth by one iota, show us plainly that giants did exist. . . ."(519)

This is very subtle irony, the ultimate object of which is difficult to determine. Certainly it is ironic that the curate, who is making fun of Don Quixote's belief in giants, should be confronted with scriptural evidence of their existence. The motivation of the curate at this particular point—the only time when he gratuitously indulges Don Quixote in his chivalric fantasies—is suspect ("merely for the pleasure of listening to such utter nonsense"), and in that sense he is a trickster quite appropriately tricked. It would nevertheless be difficult to say, without supporting evidence in other contexts, that the irony is to be carried further.

If he is the ingénu in the above exchange with the curate, Don Quixote is clearly a conscious ironist in the negotiations with Sancho in Chapter VII. At the insistence of Teresa, Sancho is trying, in a very roundabout way that reflects his own uneasiness, to come to the point of asking Don Quixote for a fixed wage, and his master is playing with the squire's linguistic problems:

56.　　"I will bet you," said Sancho, "that you understood what I meant all the time and just wanted to mix me up so that you could hear me make a lot more blunders."

"You may be right," replied Don Quixote, "but tell me, exactly what was it that Teresa said?"

"She said that I should get everything down in black and white with your Grace, to let papers talk and beards be still, since he who binds does not wrangle, and one 'take' is worth a couple of 'I'll give you's.' And I can tell you that a woman's advice is of little worth and he who won't take it is a fool."

"And so say I," observed Don Quixote. "Go on, friend Sancho, *you are in rare form today*." (550–51)

An even clearer revelation of the change in Don Quixote comes with his treatment of the "joker" Sansón Carrasco, who, as the tool of the first instance of Irony of Events in Part II, enters to offer his services as squire precisely at the moment when Don Quixote has rejected the demands of Sancho. He declines Sansón's offer in the following terms:

57.   But Heaven forbid that, to gratify my own inclinations, I should shatter this *pillar of letters and vase of learning and cut down this towering palm of the fine and liberal arts*. (553)

The excessive praise which is such a common tactic in Cervantes' irony might simply be taken here as an example of Don Quixote's usual tendency to express himself hyperbolically were it not for the internal contradiction with his characterization of Sansón a moment before as "the darling and perpetual delight of the Salamancan schools." Don Quixote knows now, as he will say in Chapter XVIII, that "the majority of people in this world are of the opinion that knights-errant never existed" (623), and he must at least suspect, in this moment of lucidity when he has just been ironic with Sancho, that Sansón is "putting him on," even though, as we are told in Chapter VII, "Carrasco . . . was their oracle" (554).

In a wonderful piece of internal contradiction in Chapter V, Sancho betrays both his eagerness to leave home again with Don Quixote and the consequent guilt he feels toward his wife.

81

58.   "What do you bring with you, friend Sancho," she
       asked, "that makes you so merry?"
       "Wife," he replied, "if it was God's will, *I'd be glad not to
       be as happy as I am.*" (538)

Though Teresa sees the contradiction ("I may be a fool, but I fail
to see how you can find pleasure in not having it"), she remains a
victim of the irony since she is merely confused and does not
perceive what Sancho's remark really reveals.

   Things have changed in the world of Don Quixote. The knight's
antagonists are now victims and objects of irony. The ingenuous
Don Quixote of Part I now coexists with an ironic Don Quixote:
the *loco* is already becoming a *cuerdo-loco*.

The Third Sally: Specific Comic Irony

In Chapter VIII the question of religious faith enters the field of
observation. Let us see how far our focus upon the irony in *Don
Quixote* can take us in the determination of the religious orientation of the novel. We can begin with the following self-portrait
offered by Sancho:

59.   It is true, I am somewhat sly, and I have certain marks of
       the rogue, but *it is all covered over with the great cloak of
       my simplicity, which is always natural and never artifi-
       cial.* (557)

His attribution to himself of a natural simplicity that covers
slyness and knavery alerts us to the irony of which Sancho is the
victim. The internal contradiction in his statement automati-
cally invalidates it. We may recall, as Sancho goes on to characterize his religious situation, a statement from Chapter XXXI of
Part I: " 'That,' observed Sancho, 'is the kind of love I have heard
the preacher say we ought to give to Our Lord, for Himself alone,
without being moved by any hope of eternal glory or fear of Hell;
but, for my part, *I prefer to love and serve Him for what He can do
for me*'" (270–71). Sancho's self-portrait in the present context
continues as follows:

60.   and *if I had no other virtue than that of* believing, as I
      always have believed, firmly and truly in God and in all
      that the holy Roman Catholic Church holds and believes,
      as well as that of *being, as I am, a mortal enemy of the
      Jews, the historians ought to have mercy on me and treat
      me well in their writings*. (557)

The internal contradiction involved in Sancho's hope that the
historian, whom he knows to be Moorish, will treat him well
because he (Sancho) hates Jews allows us to separate legitimately the two elements that he alleges in his defense. A non-
Christian "historian" could treat a faithful Christian well, as
Cervantes treats Zoraida's father well, for example, but could
scarcely be expected to sympathize with what he would have to
see as religious intolerance. A duality has thus developed which
could be represented as follows:

Sancho

1. "my simplicity, which is always natural and never artificial"	1. "*I am somewhat sly, and I have certain marks of the rogue*"
2. "we ought to [love] Our Lord without being moved by any hope of eternal glory or fear of Hell"	2. "*I prefer to love and serve Him for what He can do for me*"
3. "I always have believed, firmly and truly in God"	3. "*I am a mortal enemy of the Jews*"

Nothing in the rhetoric of the passage would seem *necessarily*
to devalue or undercut the statements on the left, except that the
first is not true in the sense that Sancho means it ("all covered
over"). It is in fact truer than he knows, as a description of his
fundamental unawareness of the contradiction. It is this rhetorical orientation that allows us to put into perspective not only the
series of conflicting values that are the subject of discussion in
the rest of the chapter but also a number of parallel elements

from previous chapters. In the case of Sancho, it seems clear that the dichotomy continues to develop as follows:

4. "we ought to become saints"	4. "and that way *we'd have the fame we are after all the sooner*": the fame attested to by "*crutches, shrouds, locks of hair, legs, and eyes made of wax*" (560–61)

A parallel division for Don Quixote is suggested by his specification, in response to Sancho, of the relationship between knight-errantry and Christianity:

61. *In confronting giants, it is the sin of pride that we slay,* even as we combat envy with generosity and goodness of heart; anger, with equanimity and a calm bearing; gluttony and an overfondness for sleep, by eating little when we do eat and by keeping long vigils: lust and lewdness, with the loyalty that we show to those whom we have made the mistresses of our affections, and sloth by going everywhere in the world in search of opportunities that may and do make of us famous knights as well as better Christians. (559)

The disparity between the struggle against pride, seen as external, and the struggle against the other vices through *self*-purification highlights precisely the object of the systematic irony directed against Don Quixote up to this point. Some parallel elements are listed below:

Don Quixote

1. "we combat envy with generosity and goodness of heart"	1. *"In confronting giants, it is the sin of pride that we slay"*
2. "It is not good for self-respecting men to be executioners [*verdugos*] of their fellow-men" (174)	2. *"[I am] executioner [verdugo] of the world's evildoers"* (*393)
3. "God in Heaven will not fail to punish the evil and reward the good" (174)	3. *"Thus we become the ministers of God on earth"* (94)

84

Sancho is, on the one hand, the candid sincere believer, and on the other, a malicious knave. Don Quixote is, on the one hand, ascetic and charitable, and on the other, arrogant and vain. His last statement on the positive side exactly characterizes the providential Irony of Events that we have seen in operation in the world of *Don Quixote*, Part I.

But the irony of Cervantes' novel is always directed primarily at the vice and not at the individual who at any given moment falls victim to it. This is consonant with Don Quixote's advice to Don Diego de Miranda to encourage his son to write satires "in the manner of Horace, in which he reprehends vice in general" (610) without singling out specific individuals. Don Quixote himself becomes, in the third sally, a conscious ironist, extremely adept at exposing the follies of others. This is one of the major differences between Parts I and II and an important component of the movement toward sanity. Don Quixote expresses the same pretended doubt as did the narrator (37) concerning the separability of the moral and the monetary:

62. "The poor man who is a man of honor (*if such a thing is possible*). . . ." (649)

He can ridicule the victim through overpraise, as he did with Sansón in (57):

63. "I can assure you," said Don Quixote at this point, "that *the sparingness and cleanliness with which Sancho eats might be inscribed and engraved on tablets of bronze, to be preserved as a lasting memorial for future ages.* I grant you that when he is hungry he appears to be a bit of a glutton. . . ." (915)

64. "Body of me!" exclaimed Don Quixote, "*how far advanced your Grace is in the Italian language*! I will lay you a good wager that you translate *piace* as *place*, *più* as *más*, *su* as *arriba*, and *giù* as *abajo*."
    "I do indeed," said the author, "for those are the proper equivalents."
    "And *I would venture to take an oath*," Don Quixote went on, "*that your Grace is not known to the world at*

85

> *large, which always is chary of rewarding men of excep-*
> *tional ability and works deserving of praise. How many*
> *talents have been lost in that way, how many geniuses have*
> *been tossed into the corner, how much of real worth has*
> *gone unappreciated!* But, for all of that, it appears to me
> that translating from one language into another ... is like
> gazing at a Flemish tapestry with the wrong side out. ...
> Moreover, translating from easy languages does not call
> for either wit or eloquence. . . ." (923)

He can be as subtle as Cervantes himself with innuendo and
insinuation:

65. "Does that hermit you are speaking of by any chance
     keep hens?" Sancho asked.
        "Few hermits are without them," said Don Quixote;
     "for those of today are not like the ones that dwelt in the
     deserts of Egypt, who clothed themselves in palm leaves
     and lived on the roots of the earth. And do not think that
     by praising the latter I am disparaging the former. What
     I mean to say is that the penances they do now cannot
     compare in rigor and harshness with those performed in
     olden times. This is not to say that they are not all of them
     good men; [*at least, I judge them to be good*]; *and if worst*
     comes to worst, the hypocrite who pretends to be good does
     less harm than the flagrant sinner." (*667)

In this kind of pretended defense of the victim, the more the
ironist talks, the worse for the victim, who ends up here a hypocrite only slightly superior to the flagrant sinner. The appearance of the "feminine sub-hermit," which is the sole justification
for the brief stop at the hermitage just after this speech, is the
icing on this particular ironic cake, a product of the collaboration
of Cervantes and Don Quixote.

We also find examples of the irony of praise for desirable qualities lacking in the victim in Don Quixote's exposure of Sancho's
weaknesses:

66. "I must say, Sancho," replied Don Quixote, "that *your*
     proverbs always come in very pat no matter what it is we
     are talking about." (567)

The most revealing example of this type occurs when Sancho declines to take Don Quixote's suggestion that Sancho himself avenge the offense his gray has suffered at the hands of the traveling players:

67. "There is no reason," replied Sancho, "why I should take vengeance on anyone; for it is not for good Christians to avenge the wrongs that are done them. . . ."
     "Since that is your resolve, *my good Sancho, my wise Sancho, [my Christian Sancho, and my sincere Sancho]*, let us leave these phantoms. . . ." (*578)

Good Sancho, which might have passed unnoticed in isolation, begins to be undercut by *wise [discreto] Sancho* since the two terms are mutually exclusive as designations of qualities which might be inferred from Sancho's remark. *Christian Sancho*, as an echo of Sancho's own word, brings stronger irony to bear, and *sincere Sancho* constitutes the climax. The internal contradiction combined with pretended agreement with the victim and capped by praise for the specific desirable quality lacking in Sancho's hypocritical statement qualify Don Quixote as a consummate ironist. He is thus at the opposite pole from the ingénu who innocently accepts what people say at face value. He is perfectly capable of perceiving the hypocrisy behind protestations of noble motives and of exposing it through irony.[19]

But Don Quixote's new perceptiveness does not preclude his continuing to be the victim of other ironies whenever he exhibits the weaknesses or vices against which the novel consistently works. He is the victim of Sancho's irony when the latter hides his deception of Don Quixote in the enchantment of Dulcinea behind the following ambiguous allusion to his own knavery:

68. But let us leave it to God, for he knows all that is to happen in this vale of tears, in this evil world of ours, where *you scarcely find anything that does not have in it some mixture of wickedness, deceit, and villainy*. (574)

19. Surely Anthony Close's keen sense of irony fails him when he takes this statement by Don Quixote literally, in "Sancho Panza: Wise Fool," p. 355.

Don Quixote continues, too, to be a target of irony, but with much less frequency and in ways that need more qualification. The single example that I have observed in Part II where Don Quixote's words might be said to betray the vanity so characteristic of him in Part I is the following exchange during Doña Rodríguez' nocturnal visit to his bedroom:

69. "Am I safe, Sir Knight?" she asked, falling back a step or two. "For I do not look upon it as very decent on your part to have left your bed."
"Lady," replied Don Quixote, "that is a question which I well might ask of you. In fact, *I do ask you if I am safe from being attacked and raped.*" (819)

In another situation, Don Quixote betrays a mixture of envy and an outraged sense of justice at Sancho's unmerited good fortune in getting his governorship:

70. "Sancho, my friend, I thank Heaven with all my heart that good Fortune should have come your way before I have met with her. I had counted upon my luck to enable me to pay you for your services, but here am I at the beginning of my adventures while *you, ahead of time and contrary to all reasonable expectation,* are seeing your desires fulfilled. . . . *You to my mind are beyond any doubt a blockhead.* . . ." (780)

What Cervantes achieves here, however, with great stylistic subtlety and psychological insight, is an ironic self-betrayal that evokes sympathy and understanding rather than blame or ridicule. The surrounding context reveals the knight's deep affection for Sancho, his appreciation of his good qualities, and his genuine desire that he succeed in the governorship, and the reader cannot but admire this transparent attempt by Don Quixote to overcome the hurt and envy which he naturally feels.

The final example of the dramatized irony of self-betrayal by Don Quixote in the third sally is similarly complex. It involves the bogus lashings of Sancho for the disenchantment of Dulcinea:

71.   "Take care, my friend, that you do not cut yourself to pieces; let there be a space between the lashes, and do not be in such haste that your breath will give out by the time you are half done; by which I mean to say, *do not lay on so stoutly that life will fail you before you have attained the desired number.*" (970)

Disarmed by the knowledge of Sancho's shameless deceit ("he had stripped the bark off any number of trees, such was the severity with which he whipped himself"), and aware of the intensity of Don Quixote's obsession with the enchantment of Dulcinea and the frustration he has felt at seeing her fate placed in the hands of Sancho, the reader can scarcely react as he did to the instances of self-betrayal by Don Quixote in Part I.

Sancho is involved more extensively in the irony commensurate with his expanded role and increased complexity and articulateness. At times he is the classic ingénu:

72.   ". . . Don Quixote de la Mancha, who rights wrongs and *gives food to the thirsty and drink to the hungry.*" (567)

73.   ". . . according to what Sansón Carrasco told me, and he at least is a bachelor of Salamanca, and *people like him can't lie, unless the fancy happens to take them or they find it very convenient to do so.*" (733)

This example counts against both Sancho and Sansón—against Sancho because the absurd reasoning exposed by the internal contradiction is part of his disingenuous self-exoneration in the matter of the enchantment of Dulcinea, and against Sansón as a reminder that he is in fact a devious trickster.

But Sancho is much more often the conscious ironist in the third sally. We have seen how he can deceive with the truth in example 68, and this is, in fact, his favorite tactic:

74.   "Who in the devil was it but me that first thought up this enchantment business! *She's as much enchanted as my father.*" (715)

89

When the "cousin" tells Don Quixote to keep his eyes open in his descent into the Cave of Montesinos for material for his book of *Transformations*, Sancho is quick to victimize the gullible "humanist":

75.   *"Leave the tambourine,"* Sancho advised him, *"to the one who knows how to play it."* (653)

In his letter to Teresa, Sancho pretends to take literally a proverb which he knows well enough to use at other times:

76.   The only thing is, I am told that after I once try it I'll be eating my hands off for it, and *if that is the case, it will not come so cheap after all*, though, to be sure, the maimed and the crippled have their benefice in the alms that they beg. (750)

Finally, he is also a practitioner of the irony of intentional ambiguity:

77.   "... it makes no difference so far as the truth of the story is concerned whether the brayers were one or the other, so long as bray they did, and *a judge can bray just as well as an alderman*." (690)

78.   *"I have seen more than one ass go up to a government*, and so it would be nothing new if I took mine with me." (734)

But if Sancho can poke ironic fun at others, he betrays his own weaknesses often enough. He reveals his excessive fondness for wine by taking literally a proverb used by the duchess in ironic praise of his eloquence:

79.   "All that the worthy Sancho has just said," remarked the duchess, "is out of Cato's maxims. . . . In short, speaking after his own manner, under a bad cloak you commonly find a good drinker."
      "Well, to tell you the truth, lady," replied Sancho, "I

never in my life have drunk from malice, though it well
may be that I have from thirst, for there's nothing of the
hypocrite in me. . . . *If a friend drinks to your health, you'd
have to have a heart of marble, wouldn't you, not to raise
your glass with his?*" (733)

He hypocritically hides his greed:

80. "*If I appear grasping, you must blame it on the love I have
for my wife and young ones.* Tell me, your Grace, how
much is each lash worth to you?" (969)

and his fear of the Squire of the Wood's nose:

81. "*Señor mío*, I beg your Grace, before you turn for the
charge, to help me up into that cork tree yonder *where I
can watch the encounter* which your Grace is going to
have with this knight *better than I can from the ground
and in a way that is much more to my liking.*" (597)

In his abrupt change of sides in the choice between Basilio and
Camacho, he reveals that a mere whiff of the aroma of Camacho's
feast can buy his support. When he first hears of the rivalry
between the two, he immediately sides with Basilio in line with
the plans he has for his daughter's marriage:

"I'd like to see the good Basilio—for I'm taking a liking to
him already—marry this lady Quiteria, and eternal
blessings—no, I mean just the opposite—on all those that
would keep true lovers apart." (630)

But when he awakens the following morning, other interests
intervene:

82. "If I am not mistaken," he said, "there is a steam and
smell coming from around that arcade that is more like
that of broiled rashers than it is like jonquils or thyme.
Faith, and a wedding that begins with such a smell ought
to be all right; there should be plenty to eat."
    "That will be enough from you, glutton," said Don

Quixote, "Come, we are going to those nuptials to see what the rejected suiter, Basilio, will do."

"Let him do what he likes," replied Sancho. "He's a poor man, and yet he is bent on marrying Quiteria. *He hasn't a cuarto to his name, and yet he'd put his head in the clouds to look for a bride.*" (636)

There is considerable ingénu irony in Part II involving other characters as well. The swordsman-licentiate, telling Don Quixote about his cousin the humanist:

83. He assured the knight that the youth would be found to be entertaining company, since he knew enough to write books of his own, *books that were printed and dedicated to princes.* (651)

The tailor on Barataria:

84. "Yesterday this good man entered my shop—for, *begging the pardon of those present,* I am a licensed tailor." (799)

The children of Don Quixote's hometown, who may or may not be ingenuously describing Rocinante and Sancho's gray:

85. "Come lads," they cried, "and see Sancho Panza's ass [*el asno de Sancho Panza*] trigged out finer than Mingo, and Don Quixote's beast [*la bestia de Don Quijote*] is skinnier than ever!" (979)

The braying aldermen:

86. *"There is not the slightest difference between you and an ass* so far as braying is concerned. . . ." (673)

Finally, Don Diego de Miranda's ingenuous response to Don Quixote's self-description puts the knight in an extremely awkward position:

87. "Thank Heaven for that book that your Grace tells me has been published concerning your true and exalted

deeds of chivalry, as it should cast into oblivion all *the
innumerable stories of fictitious knights-errant* with
which the world is filled, *greatly to the detriment of good
morals and the prejudice and discredit of legitimate his-
tories*." (606)

The conscious irony of characters who pretend agreement with
Don Quixote and Sancho of course increases in Part II, since so
many of them have read Part I. In conversation with Sancho, the
duchess manages to deceive him with the truth:

88. "Believe me, Sancho, that sportive lass was and is Dul-
     cinea del Toboso, who is *as much enchanted as the mother
     that bore her*." (732)

Don Quixote is also her victim:

89. "Dulcinea del Toboso, who ... must surely be the fairest
     creature in the world *and even in all La Mancha*." (721)

We have already seen the curate (55) and Sansón Carrasco (57,
73) on the receiving end of the irony of Don Quixote and Sancho.
Sansón, in addition, betrays his hypocrisy in conversation with
Don Antonio Moreno in Barcelona, for although he reveals that
he was defeated by Don Quixote in their first encounter, he goes
on as follows:

90. "I beg you not to disclose my secret or reveal my identity
     to Don Quixote, in order that *my well-intentioned scheme*
     may be carried out and a man of excellent judgment be
     brought back to his senses." (939)

The reader has not forgotten Sansón's comment after the first
encounter:

"To imagine that I am going back before I have given Don
Quixote a good thrashing is senseless; and what will urge
me on now is not any desire to see him recover his wits, but
rather a thirst for vengeance. ..." (602)

That he has not lost this new motive is clear from the arrogance of his challenge in the second encounter: "My lady, whoever she may be"; "today is all the time I have for the dispatching of this business." (935)

It is enormously satisfying to witness the betrayal by Altisidora of her wounded vanity when, unable to seduce Don Quixote, she briefly drops the pose of lovestruck damsel and lashes out at him:

91.   Altisidora was about to go on with her reproaches addressed to Don Quixote when he interrupted her. "Lady," he said, "I have told you many times how it grieves me that you should have fastened your affections upon me. . . ."

   Hearing this, Altisidora became angry and excited: *"By the living God, Don Codfish!"* she cried. *"Soul of a brass mortar, date-stone harder and more obdurate than an ignorant rustic when you ask him to do you a favor and he has made up his mind to the contrary! Just let me throw myself on you and I'll scratch your eyes out! Do you perhaps think, Don Vanquished, Don Cudgeled, that it was for you I died? All that you saw last night was pretense."* (966)

Moments later the "trickster tricked" regains control and reassumes the pose, "dabbing at her eyes with a handkerchief as if to wipe the tears away" (968).

The figure of the "cousin" recalls the satire of vain authors in Part I, now effected through the self-styled humanist's characterization of his work:

92.   "I have another book which I call *Supplement to Virgilius Polydorus*. It treats of the invention of things and is a very scholarly work and one that cost me much study. In it I set forth in a pleasing style, with due proof and explanation, certain things of great moment that Polydorus neglected to mention. He forgot to tell us who was the first man in the world to have a cold in the head, or the first to take unctions for the French disease, all of which I bring out most accurately, citing the authority of

more than twenty-five authors. From this your Grace
may see *how well I have labored and* may judge for yourself as to *whether or not such a work should be useful to
everyone.*" (652)

This brings us back to the narrator's ironic confusion of
pseudohistoricity and verisimilitude, of which there are even
more examples in Part II than in Part I. The fictionality of *Don
Quixote* is repeatedly brought to the foreground in different
ways. The anachronism of example 48 from Part I appears again:

93.　The close friendship that existed between the two ani-
　　　mals was a most unusual one, so remarkable indeed that
　　　it has become a tradition handed down from father to son.
　　　. . . (581)

94.　(*From this may be seen how ancient is the use of starch
　　　and of crimped ruffs as well.*) (793)

There are a number of examples of a kind of absurd specificity
which presupposes a criterion of inane historicism much like that
of the "cousin" and like that which produced the repeated resolu-
tions of the mystery of Don Quixote's real name in 19, 22, and 30:

95.　three ass-colts or fillies—the author is not specific on this
　　　point, but it seems more likely that they were she-asses,
　　　on which village girls commonly ride. *However, it is of no
　　　great importance and there is no reason why we should
　　　stop to verify so trifling a detail.* (568)

96.　a dense grove of oak or cork trees (*on this point Cid
　　　Hamete is not as precise as he usually is*). (899)

97.　five or six buckets of water (*there is some difference of
　　　opinion as to the exact number*). (621)

Sometimes the tactic involves a deadpan clarification:

98.　Don Quixote now sat down at the foot of an elm and
　　　Sancho at the foot of a beech (*for trees of this sort and
　　　others like them always have feet but no hands*). (697)

99.   And thus, amid the tears and lamentations of those present, he gave up the ghost; *that is to say, he died.* (987)

At times there is internal contradiction:

100.   It was midnight on the hour, *a little more or less.* . . . (562)

The most elaborate example of the narrator's explanations, which either do not explain or else do not convince, is the well-known elucidation of Cid Hamete's oath:

101.   Cid Hamete, the chronicler of this great history, begins the present chapter with these words: "I swear as a Catholic Christian"; which leads his translator to remark that, being a Moor as he undoubtedly was, *the author merely meant that, just as a Catholic Christian when he takes an oath swears, or is supposed to swear, to tell the truth in all that he says, so in what he himself has to set down about Don Quixote he will adhere to the truth just as* if he were taking such a Christian oath. . . . (687)

The following example seems to take many readers unawares:

102.   *They say that in the original version of the history it is stated that the interpreter did not translate the present chapter as Cid Hamete had written it,* . . . (788)

This suggestion that one can read in the original that the translator has mistranslated that original offended Clemencín's sense of order and logic: "All this at the beginning of the chapter is an unintelligible jumble. For how can one read in the original text of the story that the translator did not translate it faithfully? . . . This long and diffuse preamble could very well have been omitted. . . ." [20]

The Third Sally: General Comic Irony

With the exception of the early example of the timing of Sansón's offer to serve as Don Quixote's squire, Irony of Events in the

20. Clemencín, pp. 1765–66n1.

third sally occurs exclusively in the service of the theme of the "tricksters tricked." All of Don Quixote's principal antagonists are its victims:

103.   Sansón Carrasco

A complex chain reaction is set off by Sansón: he and Tomé Cecial disguise themselves to fool Don Quixote; Tomé's false nose frightens Sancho, who asks Don Quixote to help him climb a tree at the moment when Sansón begins his charge; Don Quixote's delay obliges Sansón to stop in mid-course; Don Quixote easily unhorses Sansón, who is occupied trying to get his horse moving again. Sansón had carelessly brought a poor mount, considering a victory over Don Quixote "easy of accomplishment" (601), thus setting himself up for ironic victimization.

Doña Rodríguez' simple-minded credulity is the vehicle for a series of revelations that embarrass and anger the duke, the duchess, and Altisidora.

104.   Altisidora

"In this girl Altisidora there is more of presumption than of beauty and more of sprightliness than of modesty. What is more, she is none too healthy. Her breath is so bad that one cannot bear to be near her for a moment...." (822)

105.   The duchess

"You are aware, Señor Don Quixote, of my lady's beauty: that complexion of hers which is like a smooth-polished sword; those cheeks of milk and carmine, one of which is like the sun while the other resembles the moon; that lightsome step with which she barely skims the ground. From all of this would it not seem that she radiates health wherever she goes? But I would have your Grace know, she may first of all thank God for it, and in the second place she may be grateful for two issues that she has, one in each leg, through which are discharged all the evil humors of which the doctors say she is full." (822)

106.   The duke

The duke of course loses the reader's esteem as a result of Doña
Rodríguez' revelation of his attitude toward her problem:

> "My lord the duke is aware of this, for I have complained to
> him not one but many times, imploring him to order that
> farmer's son to marry her, but he turns a deaf ear and
> scarcely listens to me. The reason is that the young de-
> ceiver's father is so rich; he lends the duke money and goes
> security for his debts from time to time, and so my lord does
> not wish to offend him or give him trouble of any sort." (821)

But Irony of Events, as distinguished from the dramatized irony
of self-betrayal, "needs to be completed by the discomfiture of the
victim" (Muecke, pp. 104–5), and only Altisidora and the duchess,
"filled with rage and thirsting for vengeance" (834), are listening
outside the door. And so Tosilos must fall in love with Doña
Rodríguez' daughter and concede victory to Don Quixote, leaving the duke "amazed and very angry" (876)

The dramatized irony of Sancho's performance as governor
also constitutes a clear instance of the "tricksters tricked." Contrary to the expectations of the duke and duchess and of the
reader, who has been told by the narrator to expect "two bushels
of laughter" (790),

107.   he ordered things so wisely that to this day his decrees
       are preserved in that town, under the title of *The Con-
       stitutions of the Great Governor, Sancho Panza.* (849)

Conclusions

> Each day new things are seen in this world, jests
> are turned into earnest and the jesters are mocked.
>
> (Part II, Chapter XLIX, 825)

The *victims* of irony in the third sally are:

1. the narrator (pseudovictim): 53, 54, 93, 94, 95, 96, 97, 98,
99, 100, 101, 102;

2. Don Quixote: 61, 68, 69, 70, 71, 72, 74, 87, 89; (pseudovictim): 56, 57, 62, 63, 64, 65, 66, 67;
3. Sancho: 58, 59, 60, 73, 79, 80, 81, 82, 88; (pseudovictim): 68, 74, 75, 76, 77, 78, 79, 80;
4. the curate: 55;
5. Sansón: 73, 90, 103;
6. Altisidora: 91, 104;
7. the duchess: 105, 107;
8. the duke: 106, 107;
9. the "cousin": 75, 83, 92;
10. Teresa Panza: 58;
11. the tailor: 84;
12. the alderman: 86.

The *objects* (targets) of the irony are:

1. inverisimilitude: 93, 94, 95, 96, 97, 98, 101, 102; and failure to perceive it: 87;
2. greed: 80;
3. hypocrisy: 53, 58, 59, 65, 67, 79, 80, 81, 82, 90;
4. vanity: 61, 69, 91, 92, 104, 105;
5. confusion of the moral and the monetary: 62, 106;
6. overindulgence in food and wine: 63, 79;
7. intolerance: 60;
8. those who manifest any of the above: Don Quixote 61, 69, 70, 71, 87; Sancho 58, 59, 60, 63, 67, 79, 80, 81, 82; Sansón 73, 90; Altisidora 91, 104; the duchess 105; the duke 106; hermits 65; the "cousin" 83, 92; Lope de Vega 53.
9. Avellaneda 54; Sansón 57, 73, 103; the translator 64; Sancho 66, 85; Don Quixote 72, 85; asinine judges and governors 77, 78, 86; the tailor 84.

The *ironists* are:

1. the narrator: 53, 54, 93, 94, 95, 96, 97, 98, 99, 100, 101, 102;
2. the curate: p. 568; Sansón: p. 558; the duchess: 88, 89;
3. Sancho: 68, 74, 75, 76, 77, 78;
4. Don Quixote: 56, 57, 62, 63, 64, 65, 66, 67.

Although there is a relative abundance of ingénu irony in the third sally, Don Quixote is never the ingénu except in 55. The list

of targets remains remarkably consistent. Don Quixote and Sancho have become accomplished ironists, and the knight's antagonists have become the victims and targets not only of the
irony of the two protagonists but of the Irony of Events. Sancho
is the object of considerable irony, both before and after (but not
during) the governorship.

IV. STRATEGIES OF IRONY

> O dearly beloved creatures! May the madness that
> takes us from you be turned into sound sense and
> bring us back to you once more!
>
> (Part II, Chapter XXIX, 699)

I began by posing three sets of questions.

Who are the victims and what are the objects or targets of
Cervantes' irony? The foregoing attempt to answer this question
as exhaustively as possible does not preclude the addition of
more victims and targets of ironies which I have missed or of
examples with which I might wrongly disagree, but it should at
least provide a list sufficiently comprehensive to serve as a basis
for rational discussion and disagreement.

Are there indications as to where to stop in ironic reconstruction? Is the irony *limited*? If the list of examples studied is
sufficiently complete and/or representative, and if one accepts
Booth's assertion that ironic reconstruction stops when one has
found "a convincing pattern of messages or satirical thrusts
against some belief or person or thing in the so-called real world"
(p. 140), then the answer is yes. The "convincing pattern" involves us in the third question.

Can we identify the norms implicit in the ironies sufficiently to
adumbrate the strategies behind them? Is the irony *stable*? The
consistent application of irony to a rather limited set of vices or
weaknesses that we have seen in *Don Quixote* leaves little doubt
as to the norms behind the irony. Oscar Mandel's investigation in
"The Function of the Norm in *Don Quixote*"[21] led him to single
out Don Diego de Miranda as the character who most clearly

21. "The Function of the Norm," p. 160.

100

represents the desirable norm in the novel. The vehemence, ingenuity, and persistence of opposing points of view not-withstanding,[22] my investigation supports his conclusions. In a context which, in its totality, argues for taking Don Diego seriously, and not as the ironic victim of a betrayal of hypocrisy, he says that he gives to the poor, etc., "but make no parade of my good works lest hypocrisy and vainglory, those enemies that so imperceptibly take possession of the most modest heart, should find their way into mine" (607). These are precisely the two human failings most consistently exposed through irony in *Don Quixote*. Even if one were to take the statement as ironic self-betrayal, it would constitute another example of irony based upon the exposure of these two vices.[23]

Before moving from the novel's norms to the discussion of the strategies of irony which they inform, perhaps it is appropriate here to make another point. The identification of strategies of irony helps one not only to establish the direction in which the novel moves, the process which it is engaged in actualizing or "imitating," but also to make judgments about individual instances of potential irony—Booth's point about where to stop in ironic reconstruction. Some examples: "These," he said, "are the books that ought to be printed, even though there are many of the sort, for many are the sinners these days, and an infinite number of lights are required for all those that are in darkness" (924). The idea that there is a need for more books of a type of which there are already many available, though it does not constitute internal contradiction (since there are alleged to be

22. See Percas, *Cervantes y su concepto del arte*, pp. 332–82, for a thorough recent exposition.

23. One reviewer of *Don Quixote: Hero or Fool?* (Part I) noted that my study had "nothing of the humour of the novel." I should perhaps acknowledge here that I am not unaware that *Don Quixote* is a very funny book. This chapter should, in fact, help to show where and why it is funny some of the times when it is funny, but that is not my primary purpose. Moreover, *Don Quixote* is a novel, i.e., a "represented action." It is not an apologue, a satire, or a moral tract. It is not at all my intention in this or the preceding chapters to imply that Cervantes wrote the novel in order to make any of the points which I have inferred from the punishment of vice and the reward of virtue, but simply to elucidate the values implicit in the strategies of irony that he employed.

101

many sinners in need of them), may be considered suspect. The message would be something like: "we are deluged by these 'pious' works," and it would square neatly with the perspective of, say, Heine, for whom "Cervantes at the time of the Inquisition took refuge in humorous irony to present his thoughts without exposing himself to the clutches of the familiars of the Holy Office ..." (cited by Muecke, p. 237). But Don Quixote is speaking here of *Light of the Soul*, a religious treatise by Fray Felipe de Meneses, and on his deathbed his only regret is that he hasn't the chance now to read books "that are the light of the soul," a transparent reference to that book. I cannot be sure that the initial statement is not ironic, but I cannot show that it is, and I know that if it could be shown to be ironic, then Don Quixote's deathbed statement would have to be ironic. Thus the two would imply an ironic strategy designed to satirize such books, a point that I think would be impossible to sustain.

Another example is Ricote's characterization of the expulsion of the Moriscos: "A heroic resolve, this, on the part of the great Philip III, and what unheard-of wisdom, his entrusting the task to such a one as Don Bernardino de Velasco!" (942). Ricote recognizes that Don Bernardino de Velasco, "whom his Majesty has charged with seeing to our banishment, ... tempers [justice with mercy]," and he affirms that he himself knew of

> the evil and foolish designs of our people, and for this reason it appeared to me to be a divine inspiration that led his Majesty to carry out so bold a resolution. Not that they were all to blame, for some were true Christians, but these latter were so few in number that they were unable to hold out against those that were not. [And it was not wise to harbor the serpent next to one's breast, having enemies in one's own house.] In short, and with good reason, the penalty of banishment was inflicted upon us. . . . (*863–64)

My personal inclinations lead me to want to see these passages as overpraise, ironic praise for blame—not because I see any rhetorical clues, however, but simply because I strongly disagree with the statement. To allege that the "goodness" of the individual Moriscos in the novel constitutes a clue to the contradiction implied is a bit like saying that Roque Guinart's goodness authorizes Catalonian banditry. In any event, such an allegation is undermined by Ricote's explicit acknowledgment that "some were true Christians."

My reluctant conviction that Cervantes and I disagree on the issue is confirmed by my inability to identify any clues to irony in the context, by the absence of a larger strategy of irony in the novel to which it could reasonably be linked, and by the consistency of this statement with the diatribe by Berganza in Cervantes' *Coloquio de los perros* that gives rise to the chilling rejoinder by Cipión: "A remedy has been sought for all the evils that you have noted and sketched out; I know that those you leave unmentioned are more numerous and more serious than those you speak of, and until now they haven't come up with an appropriate remedy. But our republic has very wise guardians who, seeing that Spain harbors in her breast as many vipers as there are Moriscos, with the help of God, will find for so much evil a certain, prompt and definitive solution."[24]

I would like nothing more than to be proven wrong about this and other statements with which I disagree (e.g., the esthetic censorship proposed by the curate in Part I, Chapter XLVIII), but I cannot lose sight of the fact that my disagreement with a given proposition in the novel does not justify the presumption that it is meant ironically.

The successive strategies of Cervantes' irony in the course of the novel involve a change in the field of observation (from the esthetic to the ethical or moral), a change in dominant tactics (from "impersonal" irony to "dramatized" irony), and a change in target characters (from Don Quixote to his antagonists). These are changes in emphasis: the esthetic field of observation recedes but does not disappear; impersonal irony continues to be impor-

24. *Novelas ejemplares*, vol. 2, ed. F. Rodríguez Marín (Madrid: Espasa Calpe, 1933), pp. 317–19. See also *Los trabajos de Persiles y Sigismunda*, vol. 2, ed. R. Schevill and A. Bonilla (Madrid: B. Rodríguez, 1914), pp. 116–21.

tant. Only in the case of the change of targets from Don Quixote to his antagonists does the shift finally become total, for reasons which will be discussed below. The operation of an ironic strategy, a "convincing pattern of messages," is especially evident where one finds a complementary combination of tactics. In the irony of the "tricksters tricked," for example, we have seen operating in concert dramatized irony (107), self-betrayal (91), the work of individual characters as ironists (88), and Irony of Events (103, 104, 105, 106).

The most interesting feature of the progressive strategies of irony in *Don Quixote* is that while what is being exposed and ridiculed does not really vary, the individuals who manifest the foibles do. Muecke has formulated a rule concerning the factors that govern fluctuations in the level of irony, which helps us to elucidate this fundamental aspect of the irony of *Don Quixote*: "To maintain the same level of irony the degree of disparity between the ironic opposites should be in inverse proportion to the degree of confident unawareness felt by the victim of the irony. Or, putting it another way, the irony may be made more striking either by stressing ironic incongruity or by stressing ironic innocence" (p. 32). Or, putting it yet another way, if either the disparity between the two levels or the confident unawareness diminishes, the irony is proportionally diminished. One has only to look again at those instances of irony in which Don Quixote is the target to see that, according to Muecke's Rule, the level of the irony directed at the knight is very high in the first sally and that it continues high in the second, while the third sally is characterized by a sharply reduced and progressively descending level of irony as *both* confident unawareness and the disparity between levels diminish. Don Quixote is not the target of irony at all in the last three chapters.[25] These examples confirm my conclusions in chapter 2 concerning the trajectory of Don Quixote from confident unawareness to *desengaño* and reveal that there is a corresponding reduction in the degree of

25. First sally: 20, 23, 24, 26, 29; second sally: 42, 43, 44, 45, 46, 51; third sally: 61, 69, 70, 71, 72, 85, 87. Example 85 cannot legitimately be counted against him.

disparity between the ostensible or apparent and the real levels. A further indication of the change is the fact that none of the cases in the third sally involves self-praise.

This pattern moves us away from analogies with most other comic works and suggests some rather surprising associations. Consider Paul Goodman's description of the operation of *tragic* irony: "Toward the beginning, the irony is more pointedly hostile against the self-confident protagonist; toward the reversal, it becomes more pitiful and tearful. In principle there is no irony in the resolution."[26] "Toward the reversal, it becomes more pitiful and tearful": one thinks of the series of gratuitous humiliations suffered by Don Quixote in Chapters LVIII to LXVIII of Part II, including what Unamuno called the *via crucis* of Don Quixote in Barcelona and the definitive defeat by the Knight of the White Moon. It is not, as some critics have argued, that Cervantes "hardens his pen against Don Quixote" toward the end. It is not, as Unamuno believed, or claimed to, that Cervantes did not understand his book or his protagonist. It is the process of tragic irony in operation, elevating Don Quixote beyond the reach of comic irony, curing his confident unawareness with one grinding *desengaño* after another. In the midst of this process, Don Quixote meets Roque Guinart, who tells him this:

> "It may be that through such mischances your crooked fortunes will be straightened out, seeing that Heaven, by strange and unheard-of roundabout ways that men never dreamed of, is accustomed to lift up the fallen and enrich the poor." (902–3)

He is referring, of course, to Providence—the Providence to which Lucinda, the curate, and the others referred (p. 74), the Providence behind Don Quixote's trajectory, his peripeteia. "Peripeteia," notes Frank Kermode, "has been called the equivalent, in narrative, of irony in rhetoric."[27]

A little later, it is Don Quixote's turn to console Roque:

26. Goodman, *The Structure of Literature*, p. 49.
27. Kermode, *The Sense of an Ending*, p. 18.

105

"Heaven, or, better, God, who is our physician, will provide the remedies to cure you—but not all of a sudden or through any miracle, for they usually do their healing work little by little" (908). The process of Don Quixote's *desengaño* proceeds little by little, too, for though he no longer takes inns for castles, he still believes at this point in salvation through knight-errantry, where "you will meet with so many hardships and misadventures that, if they were to be taken as a penance, they would land you in Heaven in the twinkling of an eye" (908). The irony of the internal contradiction ("little by little" versus "in the twinkling of an eye") lays bare the meaning of Don Quixote's experiences in the remaining chapters of the novel.

The world of *Don Quixote* is a world governed by divine Providence. Faithful, persevering young girls get their men (Lucinda, Dorotea), foolish or capricious ones pay for their follies or whims (Altisidora). Even a thoughtless young nobleman accustomed to satisfying his desires with impunity can be brought to see reason (Fernando). Cowardice and malice must be purged or paid for (Cardenio, Maritornes). Sincere reciprocal love and faith always triumph (Basilio and Quiteria, Clara and Luis, Zoraida and the captive). The game which Providence plays in achieving its ends is General Comic Irony. Could Don Quixote be the single exception to this complex system of rewards and punishments, the sole victim of paradoxical cosmic irony in a universe of providential benevolence and justice? The world of the novel would be shattered by such an incongruity. Don Quixote is intelligent, eloquent, chaste, steadfast, brave, idealistic, noble, vain, and egotistical. He never suffers for his virtues, but, as we have seen, he is brought through suffering to recognize and repent of his faults. This victory over himself is heroic. And those who correct or ridicule him out of their own base or frivolous motives must answer for it, just as Camila, the necessary agent of Anselmo's self-inflicted disaster, must pay for her adultery. The contribution of Cervantes' strategies of irony to this vast harmonious process seems undeniable.

4. CONCLUSIONS

I hope that the first essay in this collection elucidates the process by which the reader, finding himself increasingly drawn toward the protagonist as the novel progresses, experiences an inversely corresponding alienation from Cid Hamete, the obtuse narrator who stolidly maintains the ironic distance initially shared by the implied Cervantes and the reader. The second essay may serve as an example of how Cervantes so structured the novel as to shift the reader's ethical perspective on Don Quixote: new respect for Sancho parallels and foreshadows new respect for Don Quixote (a reversal of comic expectations), and Sancho's *desengaño* and renunciation of the governorship prefigure Don Quixote's *desengaño* and renunciation of his chivalric career.

The structural parallel complements and reinforces the effects of the stylistic and contextual devices that were shown in the first volume of *Don Quixote: Hero or Fool?* to guide the reader's shifting ethical orientation toward the protagonist. Without this kind of structural, stylistic, and contextual guidance, the novel's values would indeed remain as ambiguous as many critics insist that they are. Paul Goodman has observed that "generally, in any poem where the comic and the serious, or other ethical kinds, are mixed continually, there is required the systematic interference of the narrator to direct the reading."[1] *Don Quixote* is, of course, just such a poem. But not only has Cervantes disdained the obvious advantages of a reliable narrative commentary in the achievement of reader orientation, he has created in Cid Hamete's peculiar unreliability a powerful though subtle device for pushing the reader into the arms of the protagonist. And he has consequently created an unparalleled illusion of autonomy

1. Goodman, *The Structure of Literature*, p. 117.

in Don Quixote, who, at the same time that he proves Avellaneda's protagonist to be an imposter, demonstrates his
superiority to Cid Hamete's unworthy and inadequate concep-
tion of him. This is what Unamuno sensed in his reading.

The third and final essay in this volume identifies the
strategies of irony that reflect the system of values in the world
of *Don Quixote*. All three essays are thus designed to clarify the
reader's evolving relationship with the protagonist: the first by
exploring the consequences of the relationship between the
reader and the narrators, the second by elucidating the structural underpinnings of the evolving relationship in the parallel
Don Quixote/Sancho, and the third by including consideration of
the reader's relationship with all of the other important characters of the novel as they relate to its system of values.

The "hard" critics do not satisfy us when they interpret Part
II. The "soft" critics do not satisfy us when they interpret Part I.
Both interpretations are static at precisely the point where the
novel is dynamic. The perspectivist critics assert that Don Quixote can be seen as either hero or fool, depending upon one's
point of view. But, as we have seen, he is hero or fool depending
upon what page one is reading as one follows his journey—from
foolish vanity to heroic self-mastery—through a world governed
by a beneficent Providence.

BIBLIOGRAPHY

BIBLIOGRAPHY

Don Quixote: Hero or Fool? (Part I) was intended primarily for those who read and teach *Don Quixote* in English, and since many of my notes were allusions to or translations of criticism in Spanish, I did not include a bibliography. Although this volume is addressed to the same readers, the fact that the first volume is being used by many to whom the Spanish critics are accessible has led me to prepare the following bibliography of works cited in both volumes.

Allen, John J. *Don Quixote: Hero or Fool?* Gainesville: University of Florida Press, 1969.

Auerbach, Erich. *Mimesis: The Representation of Reality in Western Literature.* Translated by Willard Trask. Princeton: Princeton University Press, 1953.

Avalle-Arce, Juan Bautista. "Don Quijote o la vida como obra de arte." *Cuadernos Hispanoamericanos* 242 (1970):247–80. Reprinted in his *Nuevos deslindes cervantinos* (to which my citations refer), pp. 335–87. Barcelona: Ariel, 1975.

Bandera, Cesáreo. *Mimesis conflictiva. Ficción literaria y violencia en Cervantes y Calderón.* Madrid: Gredos, 1975.

Beckett, Samuel. *Waiting for Godot.* New York: Grove Press, 1954.

Bell, Aubrey F. G. *Cervantes.* Norman: University of Oklahoma Press, 1947.

Bergel, Lienhard. "Cervantes in Germany." In *Cervantes across the Centuries*, edited by Angel Flores and M. J. Benardete. New York: Dryden Press, 1947.

Booth, Wayne C. *The Rhetoric of Fiction.* Chicago: University of Chicago Press, 1961.

———. *A Rhetoric of Irony.* Chicago: University of Chicago Press, 1974.

———. "The Self-Conscious Narrator in Comic Fiction before *Tristram Shandy.*" *PMLA* 67 (1952): 163–85.

Brenan, Gerald. *The Literature of the Spanish People.* New York: Meridian Books, 1957.

Calderón de la Barca, Pedro. *Life is a Dream.* Translated by William E. Colford. Great Neck, N.Y.: Barron's Educational Series, 1958.

Casalduero, Joaquín. *Sentido y forma del "Quijote."* Madrid: Insula, 1966.

Cassou, Jean. "An Introduction to Cervantes." In *Cervantes across the Centuries*, edited by Angel Flores and M. J. Benardete. New York: Dryden Press, 1947.

Castro, Américo. *Cervantes y los casticismos españoles.* Barcelona-Madrid: Alfaguara, 1966.

113

———. "Como veo ahora el *Quijote*." In *El ingenioso hidalgo don Quijote de la Mancha*. Madrid: E.M.E.S.A., 1971.

———. *Hacia Cervantes*. 3d ed. Madrid: Taurus, 1967.

———. "Incarnation in *Don Quixote*." Translated by Zenia Sacks Da Silva. In *Cervantes across the Centuries*, edited by Angel Flores and M. J. Benardete. New York: Dryden Press, 1947.

———. "Prólogo." In *El ingenioso hidalgo don Quijote de la Mancha*. Mexico: Porrúa, 1960.

Cejador y Frauca, Julio. *La lengua de Cervantes*. 2 vols. Madrid: Jaime Ratés, 1905–6.

Cervantes Saavedra, Miguel de. *The Ingenious Gentleman Don Quixote de la Mancha*. Translated by Samuel Putnam. New York: Viking, 1949.

Chambers, Leland. "Structure and the Search for Truth in the *Quijote*." *Hispanic Review* 35 (1967): 309–26.

Clemencín, Diego, ed. *El ingenioso hidalgo Don Quijote de la Mancha*. Madrid: Castilla, 1966.

Close, Anthony J. "*Don Quixote* and the 'Intentionalist Fallacy.'" *British Journal of Aesthetics* 12 (1972): 19–39.

———. "Don Quixote as a Burlesque Hero: A Re-constructed Eighteenth-Century View." *Forum for Modern Language Studies* 10 (1974): 365–78.

———. "Don Quixote's Love for Dulcinea: A Study of Cervantine Irony." *Bulletin of Hispanic Studies* 50 (1973): 237–55.

———. *The Romantic Approach to "Don Quixote."* Cambridge: Cambridge University Press, 1978.

———. "Sancho Panza: Wise Fool." *Modern Language Review* 68 (1973): 344–57.

Crane, Ronald S. "The Plot of Tom Jones." In *Essays on the Eighteenth-Century Novel*, edited by R. D. Spector. Bloomington: University of Indiana Press, 1965.

Crocker, Lester G. "*Don Quijote*, Epic of Frustration." *Romanic Review* 42 (1951): 177–88.

Durán, Manuel. *La ambigüedad en el "Quijote."* Xalapa, Mexico: Universidad veracruzana, 1960.

Efron, Arthur. *Don Quixote and the Dulcineated World*. Austin: University of Texas Press, 1971.

El Saffar, Ruth S. "The Function of the Fictional Narrator in *Don Quijote*." *Modern Language Notes* 83 (1968): 164–77.

Forcione, Alban K. *Cervantes' Christian Romance: A Study of "Persiles y Sigismunda."* Princeton: Princeton University Press, 1972.

García Puertas, Manuel. *Cervantes y la crisis del renacimiento español*. Montevideo: Universidad de la República, 1962.

Girard, René. *Mensonge romantique et vérité romanesque*. Paris: Bernard Grasset, 1961.

Goodman, Paul. *The Structure of Literature*. Chicago: University of Chicago Press, 1962.

Gonthier, Denys. *El drama psicológico del "Quijote."* Madrid: Studium, 1962.

Green, Otis H. *Spain and the Western Tradition: The Castilian Mind in Literature from "El Cid" to Calderón*. 4 vols. Madison: University of Wisconsin Press, 1966.

Haley, George, "The Narrator in *Don Quijote*: Maese Pedro's Puppet Show." *Modern Language Notes* 80 (1965): 145–65.

Hartman, Geoffrey. "Structuralism: The Anglo-American Adventure." *Yale French Studies* 36–37 (1966): 148–68.

Hatzfeld, Helmut. *El "Quijote" como obra de arte del lenguaje*. 2d Spanish ed., revised and augmented. Madrid: Consejo Superior de Investigaciones Científicas, 1966.

———. *Estudios sobre el barroco*. Madrid: Gredos, 1964.

————. "Results from *Quijote* Criticism since 1947." *Anales Cervantinos* 2 (1952): 129–57.

Highet, Gilbert. *The Anatomy of Satire*. Princeton: Princeton University Press, 1962.

Kellogg, Robert. See Scholes.

Kermode, Frank. *The Sense of an Ending*. Reprint of 1967 ed. London: Oxford University Press, 1970.

Knowles, Edwin. "Cervantes and English Literature." In *Cervantes across the Centuries*, edited by Angel Flores and M. J. Benardete. New York: Dryden Press, 1947.

Knox, Norman. "On the Classification of Ironies." *Modern Philology* 70 (1972–73): 53–62.

Levin, Harry. "Cervantes and *Moby Dick*." In *Cervantes across the Centuries*, edited by Angel Flores and M. J. Benardete. New York: Dryden Press, 1947.

Madariaga, Salvador de. *"Don Quixote": An Introductory Essay in Psychology*. London: Oxford University Press, 1961.

Mandel, Oscar. "The Function of the Norm in *Don Quixote*." *Modern Philology* 55 (1957–58): 154–63.

Mañach, Jorge. *Examen del quijotismo*. Buenos Aires: Editorial Sudamericano, 1950.

Marías, Julián. "Prólogo." In Denys Gonthier, q.v.

Moreno Baez, Enrique. "Arquitectura del *Quijote*." *Revista de Filología Española* 32 (1948): 269–85.

Muecke, Douglas C. *The Compass of Irony*. London: Methuen, 1969.

————. *Irony*. The Critical Idiom, no. 13, John D. Jump, general editor. London: Methuen, 1970.

Murillo, L. A. "Cervantic Irony: The Problem for Literary Criticism." In *Homenaje a Rodrigues Moñino*. 2 vols. Madrid: Castalia, 1966.

Nabokov, Vladimir. *King, Queen, Knave*. Translated by Dmitri Nabokov. New York: McGraw-Hill, 1968.

Nelson, Lowry, Jr. "The Fictive Reader and Literary Self-Reflexiveness." In *The Disciplines of Criticism*, edited by Peter Demetz, Thomas Green, and Lowry Nelson, Jr. New Haven: Yale University Press, 1968.

Ortega y Gasset, José. *Meditaciones del "Quijote."* 3d ed. Madrid: Revista de Occidente, 1956.

Parker, Alexander A. "El concepto de la verdad en el *Quijote*." *Revista de Filología Española* 32 (1948): 287–305.

Percas de Ponseti, Helena. *Cervantes y su concepto del arte*. 2 vols. Madrid: Gredos, 1975.

Predmore, Richard L. *The World of "Don Quixote."* Cambridge: Harvard University Press, 1967.

Rico, Francisco. *La novela picaresca y el punto de vista*. Barcelona: Seix Barral, 1969.

Riley, Edward C. *Cervantes's Theory of the Novel*. Oxford: Clarendon Press, 1962.

————. "'El alba bella que las perlas cría': Dawn Description in the Novels of Cervantes." *Bulletin of Hispanic Studies* 33 (1956): 125–37.

————. "Three Versions of Don Quixote." *Modern Language Review* 68 (1973): 807–19.

————. "Who's Who in *Don Quixote*? Or an Approach to the Problem of Identity." *Modern Language Notes* 81 (1961): 113–30.

Riley, Edward C., and Avalle-Arce, Juan Bautista. *"Don Quijote."* In *Suma cervantina*, edited by Edward C. Riley and Juan Bautista Avalle-Arce. London: Támesis, 1973.

Riquer, Martín de, ed. *Don Quijote de la Mancha*. Barcelona: Juventud, 1966.

BIBLIOGRAPHY

Rosales, Luis. *Cervantes y la libertad*. 2 vols. Madrid: Gráficas Valera, 1960.
Rosenblat, Angel. "La lengua de Cervantes." In *Cervantes*. Caracas: Universidad Central, 1949.
Russell, P. E. "'Don Quixote' as a Funny Book." *Modern Language Review* 64 (1969): 312–26.
Sacks, Sheldon. *Fiction and the Shape of Belief*. Berkeley: University of California Press, 1967.
Scholes, Robert, and Kellogg, Robert. *The Nature of Narrative*. New York: Oxford University Press, 1966.
Schürr, Friedrich. "Cervantes y el romanticismo." *Anales Cervantinos* 1 (1951): 41–70.
Spitzer, Leo. "Linguistic Perspectivism in the *Don Quijote*." In *Linguistics and Literary History: Essays in Stylistics*. Princeton: Princeton University Press, 1948.
Stagg, Geoffrey L. "El sabio Cide Hamete Venengeli." *Bulletin of Hispanic Studies* 33 (1956): 219–25.
———. "Revision in *Don Quijote*, Part I." In *Hispanic Studies in Honor of Ignacio González Llubera*, edited by Frank Pierce. Oxford: The Dolphin Book Co., 1959.
Swabey, Marie Collins. *Comic Laughter: A Philosophical Essay*. New Haven and London: Yale University Press, 1961.
Tave, Stuart. *The Amiable Humorist*. Chicago: University of Chicago Press, 1960.
Torrente Ballester, Gonzalo. *El "Quijote" como juego*. Madrid: Guadarrama, 1975.
Unamuno, Miguel de. *Vida de don Quijote y Sancho*. Madrid: Espasa Calpe, 1956.
Valbuena Prat, Angel. *Historia de la literatura española*. 3 vols. Barcelona: Editorial Gustava Fili, 1957.
Van Doren, Mark. *Don Quixote's Profession*. New York: Columbia University Press, 1958.
Varo, Carlos. *Génesis y evolución del "Quijote"*. Madrid: Alcalá, 1968.
Wardropper, Bruce W. "The Pertinence of 'El curioso impertinente.'" *PMLA* 72 (1957): 587–600.

116

INDEX

The index covers Parts 1 and 2 of *Don Quixote, Hero or Fool?*; italic numbers refer to Part 2.

117

UNIVERSITY OF FLORIDA MONOGRAPHS

Humanities

No. 1: *Uncollected Letters of James Gates Percival*, edited by Harry R. Warfel

No. 2: *Leigh Hunt's Autobiography: The Earliest Sketches*, edited by Stephen F. Fogle

No. 3: *Pause Patterns in Elizabethan and Jacobean Drama*, by Ants Oras

No. 4: *Rhetoric and American Poetry of the Early National Period*, by Gordon E. Bigelow

No. 5: *The Background of* The Princess Casamassima, by W. H. Tilley

No. 6: *Indian Sculpture in the John and Mable Ringling Museum of Art*, by Roy C. Craven, Jr.

No. 7: *The Cestus. A Mask*, edited by Thomas B. Stroup

No. 8: Tamburlaine, Part I, *and Its Audience*, by Frank B. Fieler

No. 9: *The Case of John Darrell: Minister and Exorcist*, by Corinne Holt Rickert

No. 10: *Reflections of the Civil War in Southern Humor*, by Wade H. Hall

No. 11: *Charles Dodgson, Semeiotician*, by Daniel F. Kirk

No. 12: *Three Middle English Religious Poems*, edited by R. H. Bowers

No. 13: *The Existentialism of Miguel de Unamuno*, by José Huertas-Jourda

No. 14: *Four Spiritual Crises in Mid-Century American Fiction*, by Robert Detweiler

No. 15: *Style and Society in German Literary Expressionism*, by Egbert Krispyn

No. 16: *The Reach of Art: A Study in the Prosody of Pope*, by Jacob H. Adler

No. 17: *Malraux, Sartre, and Aragon as Political Novelists*, by Catherine Savage

No. 18: *Las Guerras Carlistas y el Reinado Isabelino en la Obra de Ramón del Valle-Inclán*, por María Dolores Lado

No. 19: *Diderot's* Vie de Sénèque: A Swan Song Revised, by Douglas A. Bonneville

No. 20: *Blank Verse and Chronology in Milton*, by Ants Oras

No. 21: *Milton's Elisions*, by Robert O. Evans

No. 22: *Prayer in Sixteenth-Century England*, by Faye L. Kelly

No. 23: *The Strangers: The Tragic World of Tristan L'Hermite*, by Claude K. Abraham

No. 24: *Dramatic Uses of Biblical Allusion in Marlowe and Shakespeare*, by James H. Sims

No. 25: *Doubt and Dogma in Maria Edgeworth*, by Mark D. Hawthorne